# ABOUT MATH SUCCESS

Welcome to Rainbow Bridge Publishing's *Math Success Grade 6*. *Math Success Grade 6* provides students with focused practice to help develop and reinforce math skills in areas appropriate for sixth-grade students. *Math Success Grade 6* uses addition and subtraction; multiplication and division; fractions, decimals, and percents; algebra; geometry; word problems; and other skills important to mathematical development. In accordance with NCTM (National Council of Teachers of Mathematics) standards, exercises are grade-level appropriate with clear instructions to guide each lesson. Activities help students develop mathematical skills and give students confidence in their ability to work with numbers.

Editors . . . . . . . . . . . . . . . . . . . . . . . . . . . . . . . . . . . . .Amy Gamble, JulieAnna Kirsch
Cover and Layout Design . . . . . . . . . . . . . . . . . . . . . . . . . . . . . . . Chasity Rice
Inside Illustrations. . . . . . . . . . . . . . . . . . . . . . . . . . . . . . . . . . . . Chasity Rice
Cover Photo. . . . . . . . . . . . . . . . . Images used under license from Shutterstock, Inc.

Printed in the USA • All rights reserved.                    ISBN 978-1-60418-047-3

# TABLE OF CONTENTS

# TABLE OF CONTENTS

**Solve each problem.**

A.
$$8 + 3$$   $$7 + 9$$   $$5 + 6$$   $$3 + 4$$   $$9 + 5$$   $$8 + 6$$

B.
$$13 - 8$$   $$17 - 9$$   $$10 - 3$$   $$15 - 7$$   $$9 - 5$$   $$16 - 8$$

C.
$$6 \times 8$$   $$7 \times 4$$   $$5 \times 9$$   $$8 \times 7$$   $$9 \times 3$$   $$4 \times 4$$

D.
$$7)\overline{63}$$   $$8)\overline{64}$$   $$9)\overline{81}$$   $$4)\overline{32}$$   $$6)\overline{42}$$   $$7)\overline{21}$$

E.
$$3,281 + 1,952$$   $$509 + 425$$   $$198\ 25 + 112$$   $$62,523 - 13,145$$   $$5,389 - 2,760$$   $$2,001 - 546$$

F.
$$2,937 \times 8$$   $$69 \times 54$$   $$332 \times 65$$   $$483 \times 367$$   $$69,512 \times 4$$   $$3,135 \times 789$$

G.
$$6)\overline{468}$$   $$7)\overline{2,307}$$   $$52)\overline{19,843}$$   $$16)\overline{4,235}$$   $$384)\overline{1,938}$$   $$697)\overline{57,201}$$

**Write an equivalent fraction for each fraction.**

A.  $\dfrac{2}{3} =$  $\dfrac{3}{4} =$  $\dfrac{2}{5} =$  $\dfrac{5}{7} =$  $\dfrac{1}{2} =$  $\dfrac{7}{8} =$

**Write each fraction in simplest form.**

B.  $\dfrac{21}{30} =$  $\dfrac{2}{8} =$  $\dfrac{12}{48} =$  $\dfrac{18}{27} =$  $\dfrac{25}{60} =$  $\dfrac{16}{32} =$

**Use >, <, or = to compare each pair of fractions.**

C.  $\dfrac{3}{8}\ \square\ \dfrac{1}{3}$  $\dfrac{1}{4}\ \square\ \dfrac{3}{8}$  $\dfrac{7}{10}\ \square\ \dfrac{4}{15}$  $\dfrac{3}{5}\ \square\ \dfrac{4}{15}$

**Write each improper fraction as a mixed number. Write each mixed number as an improper fraction. Simplify if possible.**

D.  $\dfrac{49}{6} =$  $\dfrac{62}{12} =$  $3\dfrac{1}{5} =$  $6\dfrac{9}{10} =$  $\dfrac{13}{3} =$  $12\dfrac{5}{8} =$

**Solve each problem. Simplify if possible.**

E.  $\dfrac{6}{7} + \dfrac{1}{7} =$  $\dfrac{3}{10} + \dfrac{1}{10} =$  $\dfrac{12}{15} - \dfrac{7}{15} =$

F.  $\dfrac{11}{12} - \dfrac{7}{12} =$  $\dfrac{4}{9} + \dfrac{2}{9} =$  $\dfrac{5}{6} + \dfrac{3}{6} =$

G.  $\begin{array}{r} 9\dfrac{9}{10} \\ -\ 2\dfrac{3}{10} \\ \hline \end{array}$  $\begin{array}{r} 6\dfrac{2}{5} \\ +\ 1\dfrac{1}{5} \\ \hline \end{array}$  $\begin{array}{r} 7\dfrac{7}{8} \\ -\ 3\dfrac{3}{8} \\ \hline \end{array}$  $\begin{array}{r} 1\dfrac{3}{4} \\ +\ 1\dfrac{3}{4} \\ \hline \end{array}$

**Solve each problem. Simplify if possible.**

A.

$$8\frac{2}{9}$$
$$-6\frac{7}{9}$$

$$13\frac{3}{5}$$
$$-8\frac{4}{5}$$

$$21\frac{1}{4}$$
$$-19\frac{3}{4}$$

$$4\frac{5}{6}$$
$$+2\frac{3}{4}$$

$$8\frac{5}{9}$$
$$+7\frac{2}{3}$$

B.

$$\frac{2}{3}$$
$$+\frac{1}{4}$$

$$\frac{3}{8}$$
$$-\frac{1}{16}$$

$$\frac{1}{2}$$
$$-\frac{3}{10}$$

$$\frac{4}{7}$$
$$-\frac{1}{3}$$

$$\frac{3}{5}$$
$$-\frac{1}{20}$$

C. $\frac{5}{7} \times \frac{3}{4} =$

$3\frac{3}{10} \div \frac{1}{9} =$

$\frac{6}{15} \div \frac{3}{8} =$

$2\frac{2}{7} \times 1\frac{1}{2} =$

D. $\frac{7}{9} \div \frac{2}{5} =$

$5 \div \frac{4}{5} =$

$\frac{2}{3} \div \frac{3}{7} =$

$8\frac{1}{3} \div 2\frac{1}{4} =$

**Solve the problem.**

E. Two-thirds of the students in Mrs. Dalton's class have pets. If there are 24 students in the class, how many students have pets?

**MATH SUCCESS** RB-904108

## Solve each problem.

| A. | 8.29<br>+ 2.16 | 23.25<br>+ 9.75 | 93.2<br>0.052<br>+ 12.79 | 10.589<br>+ 6.009 | 0.708<br>12<br>+ 348.5 |
|----|----|----|----|----|----|
| B. | 7.68<br>− 5.19 | 135.3<br>− 98.7 | 37.05<br>− 14.99 | 66.7<br>− 1.954 | 5<br>− 0.8 |
| C. | 0.8<br>x  3 | 3.26<br>x  14 | 0.92<br>x  1.5 | 4.18<br>x  37 | 24.99<br>x  0.52 |
| D. | $6\overline{)5.88}$ | $8\overline{)10.4}$ | $1.3\overline{)3.12}$ | $0.46\overline{)1.794}$ |
| E. | 0.103<br>x 0.005 | 0.0096<br>x  0.37 | $4\overline{)2.6}$ | $58\overline{)0.522}$ |

## Write each fraction as a decimal.

F.  $\dfrac{7}{10} =$    $\dfrac{23}{25} =$    $3\dfrac{1}{5} =$    $4\dfrac{40}{250} =$    $\dfrac{5}{8} =$

## Write each fraction or decimal as a percent.

G.  $\dfrac{1}{4} =$    $\dfrac{72}{100} =$    $\dfrac{27}{50} =$    $0.99 =$    $0.08 =$

## Solve the problem.

H.  Sarah bought a dress on Saturday. The dress was originally $78.00, but she bought it on sale for 20% off. How much did Sarah pay for the dress?

**Find each rule. Complete each pattern.**

A.    3, 9, 4, 10, 5, ____ , ____ , ____

rule: _____

2, 6, 7, 21, 22, ____ , ____ , ____

rule: _____

B.

| x | 1 | 2 | 3 | 4 | 5 | 6 | 7 |
|---|---|---|---|---|---|---|---|
| y | 8 | 9 | 10 | | | | |

rule: _____

| x | 4 | 6 | 8 | 10 | 12 | 14 | 16 |
|---|---|---|---|----|----|----|----|
| y | 2 | 3 | 4 | | | | |

rule: _____

**Solve each problem to find the variable.**

C.    $c + 7 = 13$          $g - 19 = 37$          $d \cdot 4 = 40$          $b \div 7 = 7$

D.    $\dfrac{7}{8} = \dfrac{n}{64}$          $\dfrac{p}{18} = \dfrac{4}{9}$          $\dfrac{y}{5} = \dfrac{15}{25}$          $\dfrac{13}{14} = \dfrac{39}{k}$

**Find each mean, median, mode, and range.**

E.    25, 62, 39, 45, 25

mean: _____          mode: _____

median: _____          range: _____

5, 5, 6, 9, 3, 6, 4, 6

mean: _____          mode: _____

median: _____          range: _____

**Write the equivalent measurement.**

F.    3 ft. = _____ in.          8 qt. = _____ gal          4 lb. = _____ oz.

G.    500 cm = _____ m          6 kg = _____ g          7,000 mL = _____ L

**Identify each type of triangle as *acute*, *obtuse*, or *right*. Then, find its area.**

H.    5 in.          4 in.

triangle: _____

area: _____

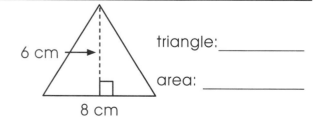

6 cm          8 cm

triangle: _____

area: _____

# DIAGNOSTIC TEST ANALYSIS

After you review students' diagnostic tests, match those problems with incorrect answers to the suggested review pages below. Giving students extra practice and supervision in these trouble areas will help students strengthen their math skills overall.

**Diagnostic Test 1**

**Problems A–B**
Addition and Subtraction Facts
Review Pages: 10, 13, 16, 18–19

**Problems C–D**
Multiplication and Division Facts
Review Pages: 20, 24, 28, 30–31

**Problem E**
2-, 3-, 4-, and 5-Digit Addition and Subtraction
Review Pages: 11–12, 14–19

**Problem F**
2-, 3-, 4-, and 5-Digit by 1- and 2-Digit
    Multiplication
Review Pages: 21–23, 28, 30–31

**Problem G**
Dividing by 1-, 2-, and 3-Digit Divisors
Review Pages: 25–31

**Diagnostic Test 2**

**Problems A–B**
Equivalent Fractions and Simplest Form
Review Pages: 33, 35, 41–42

**Problem C**
Comparing Fractions
Review Pages: 38, 41–42

**Problem D**
Writing Mixed Numbers and
    Improper Fractions
Review Pages: 43–44, 54–55

**Problems E–F**
Adding and Subtracting Fractions with
    Like Denominators
Review Pages: 45, 54–55

**Problem G**
Adding and Subtracting Mixed Numbers
    with Like Denominators
Review Pages: 46–47, 54–55

**Diagnostic Test 3**

**Problems A–B**
Adding and Subtracting Mixed Numbers
Review Pages: 46–47, 50–51, 54–55

**Problems C–D**
Multiplying and Dividing Fractions and
    Mixed Numbers
Review Pages: 56, 58–59, 62–65, 67–73

**Problem E**
Finding Fractions of Numbers
Review Pages: 61, 64

**Diagnostic Test 4**

**Problems A–B**
Adding and Subtracting Decimals
Review Pages: 74–80

**Problem C**
Multiplying Decimals
Review Pages: 82–83, 85–88

**Problem D**
Dividing Decimals
Review Pages: 89, 92–96

**Problem E**
Multiplying and Dividing across Zeros
Review Pages: 84, 87–88, 91, 93–96

**Problem F**
Changing Fractions to Decimals
Review Page: 97

**Problem G**
Changing Fractions and Decimals to Percents
Review Pages 99–100

**Problem H**
Finding Discounts and Sale Prices
Review Page: 103

**Diagnostic Test 5**

**Problem A**
Number Patterns
Review Pages: 104–106

**Problem B**
Tables
Review Page: 107

**Problem C**
Solving for Variables
Review Pages: 108–109

**Problem D**
Equal Ratios
Review Page: 114

**Problem E**
Mean, Median, Mode, and Range
Review Page: 111

**Problems F–G**
Standard and Metric Measurement
Review Pages: 116–117

**Problem H**
Classifying Triangles by Their Angles and
    Angles of Triangles
Review Pages: 119–120

9

# ADDITION FACTS REVIEW

**Solve each problem.**

A.
$$\begin{array}{r}5\\+2\\\hline\end{array}\qquad\begin{array}{r}8\\+6\\\hline\end{array}\qquad\begin{array}{r}3\\+8\\\hline\end{array}\qquad\begin{array}{r}2\\+1\\\hline\end{array}\qquad\begin{array}{r}6\\+4\\\hline\end{array}\qquad\begin{array}{r}9\\+6\\\hline\end{array}\qquad\begin{array}{r}1\\+5\\\hline\end{array}$$

B.
$$\begin{array}{r}8\\+9\\\hline\end{array}\qquad\begin{array}{r}6\\+2\\\hline\end{array}\qquad\begin{array}{r}4\\+8\\\hline\end{array}\qquad\begin{array}{r}2\\+2\\\hline\end{array}\qquad\begin{array}{r}9\\+1\\\hline\end{array}\qquad\begin{array}{r}2\\+3\\\hline\end{array}\qquad\begin{array}{r}4\\+4\\\hline\end{array}$$

C.
$$\begin{array}{r}9\\+9\\\hline\end{array}\qquad\begin{array}{r}4\\+7\\\hline\end{array}\qquad\begin{array}{r}7\\+3\\\hline\end{array}\qquad\begin{array}{r}6\\+9\\\hline\end{array}\qquad\begin{array}{r}3\\+9\\\hline\end{array}\qquad\begin{array}{r}7\\+9\\\hline\end{array}\qquad\begin{array}{r}2\\+4\\\hline\end{array}$$

D.
$$\begin{array}{r}7\\+5\\\hline\end{array}\qquad\begin{array}{r}3\\+5\\\hline\end{array}\qquad\begin{array}{r}6\\+8\\\hline\end{array}\qquad\begin{array}{r}8\\+4\\\hline\end{array}\qquad\begin{array}{r}9\\+7\\\hline\end{array}\qquad\begin{array}{r}6\\+3\\\hline\end{array}\qquad\begin{array}{r}9\\+8\\\hline\end{array}$$

E.
$$\begin{array}{r}4\\+5\\\hline\end{array}\qquad\begin{array}{r}7\\+2\\\hline\end{array}\qquad\begin{array}{r}3\\+1\\\hline\end{array}\qquad\begin{array}{r}7\\+8\\\hline\end{array}\qquad\begin{array}{r}9\\+5\\\hline\end{array}\qquad\begin{array}{r}4\\+9\\\hline\end{array}\qquad\begin{array}{r}7\\+7\\\hline\end{array}$$

F.
$$\begin{array}{r}9\\+4\\\hline\end{array}\qquad\begin{array}{r}8\\+1\\\hline\end{array}\qquad\begin{array}{r}7\\+6\\\hline\end{array}\qquad\begin{array}{r}8\\+3\\\hline\end{array}\qquad\begin{array}{r}2\\+9\\\hline\end{array}\qquad\begin{array}{r}1\\+4\\\hline\end{array}\qquad\begin{array}{r}3\\+3\\\hline\end{array}$$

G.
$$\begin{array}{r}4\\+2\\\hline\end{array}\qquad\begin{array}{r}8\\+8\\\hline\end{array}\qquad\begin{array}{r}5\\+8\\\hline\end{array}\qquad\begin{array}{r}6\\+6\\\hline\end{array}\qquad\begin{array}{r}10\\+6\\\hline\end{array}\qquad\begin{array}{r}5\\+6\\\hline\end{array}\qquad\begin{array}{r}1\\+3\\\hline\end{array}$$

H.
$$\begin{array}{r}2\\+8\\\hline\end{array}\qquad\begin{array}{r}3\\+4\\\hline\end{array}\qquad\begin{array}{r}5\\+5\\\hline\end{array}\qquad\begin{array}{r}6\\+5\\\hline\end{array}\qquad\begin{array}{r}5\\+7\\\hline\end{array}\qquad\begin{array}{r}7\\+4\\\hline\end{array}\qquad\begin{array}{r}3\\+7\\\hline\end{array}$$

**MATH SUCCESS** RB-904108

## 2-, 3-, 4-, AND 5-DIGIT ADDITION WITH REGROUPING

796 + 175

Add the ones. Regroup 11 ones as 1 ten, 1 one.

Add the tens. Regroup 17 tens as 1 hundred, 7 tens.

Add the hundreds.

```
    1
  7 9 6
+   1 7 5
        1
```

```
  1 1
  7 9 6
+   1 7 5
      7 1
```

```
  1 1
  7 9 6
+   1 7 5
    9 7 1
```

**Solve each problem.**

A.
| 45 | 329 | 673 | 471 | 923 | 357 |
|---|---|---|---|---|---|
| + 26 | + 472 | + 491 | + 82 | + 523 | + 193 |

B.
| 518 | 793 | 437 | 530 | 507 | 6,429 |
|---|---|---|---|---|---|
| + 276 | + 189 | + 825 | + 986 | + 28 | + 2,538 |

C.
| 1,768 | 1,892 | 3,576 | 7,145 | 1,482 | 8,598 |
|---|---|---|---|---|---|
| + 351 | + 2,751 | + 763 | + 9,374 | + 4,209 | + 5,305 |

D.
| 4,592 | 3,572 | 2,801 | 27,304 | 21,450 | 10,325 |
|---|---|---|---|---|---|
| + 7,009 | + 6,490 | + 7,955 | + 55,476 | + 74,607 | + 42,904 |

E.
| 35,964 | 36,832 | 21,936 | 41,874 | 25,953 | 84,767 |
|---|---|---|---|---|---|
| + 81,178 | + 22,597 | + 11,235 | + 32,297 | + 45,438 | + 22,354 |

# COLUMN ADDITION WITH REGROUPING

5,446 + 2,339 + 7,628

Add the ones.
Regroup 23 ones
as 2 tens, 3 ones.

Add the tens.
Regroup 11 tens as
1 hundred, 1 ten.

Add the hundreds.
Regroup
14 hundreds as
1 thousand,
4 hundreds.

Add the thousands.

```
    2
 5 , 4 4 6
 2 , 3 3 9
+7 , 6 2 8
         3
```

```
   1  2
 5 , 4 4 6
 2 , 3 3 9
+7 , 6 2 8
       1 3
```

```
  1  1  2
 5 , 4 4 6
 2 , 3 3 9
+7 , 6 2 8
     4 1 3
```

```
  1  1  2
 5 , 4 4 6
 2 , 3 3 9
+7 , 6 2 8
 1 5 , 4 1 3
```

## Solve each problem.

A.
| 82 | 46 | 186 | 266 | 452 | 547 |
| 28 | 27 | 355 | 275 | 397 | 218 |
| + 33 | + 35 | + 437 | + 123 | + 224 | + 193 |

B.
| 115 | 627 | 18 | 188 | 208 | 664 |
| 238 | 100 | 153 | 547 | 465 | 136 |
| 169 | 36 | 387 | 136 | 184 | 128 |
| + 54 | + 75 | + 434 | + 262 | + 922 | + 342 |

C.
| 1,644 | 2,345 | 3,651 | 5,246 | 1,565 | 3,437 |
| 1,065 | 1,127 | 2,048 | 3,254 | 1,040 | 2,059 |
| + 2,099 | + 2,269 | + 1,192 | + 2,108 | + 2,371 | + 3,128 |

D.
| 2,568 | 1,308 | 15,724 | 32,264 | 3,975 | 6,572 |
| 2,643 | 6,794 | 71,283 | 40,272 | 8,215 | 3,225 |
| + 2,345 | + 2,142 | + 28,239 | + 14,718 | 1,246 | 4,257 |
|  |  |  |  | + 4,078 | + 9,219 |

MATH SUCCESS RB-904108

# SUBTRACTION FACTS REVIEW

**Solve each problem.**

| | | | | | | |
|---|---|---|---|---|---|---|
| A. | 18<br>− 9 | 8<br>− 5 | 10<br>− 1 | 15<br>− 8 | 14<br>− 5 | 13<br>− 9 | 16<br>− 8 |

| | | | | | | |
|---|---|---|---|---|---|---|
| B. | 13<br>− 4 | 9<br>− 1 | 13<br>− 6 | 11<br>− 3 | 5<br>− 1 | 12<br>− 7 | 6<br>− 3 |

| | | | | | | |
|---|---|---|---|---|---|---|
| C. | 9<br>− 5 | 11<br>− 7 | 10<br>− 3 | 15<br>− 9 | 11<br>− 5 | 14<br>− 8 | 6<br>− 4 |

| | | | | | | |
|---|---|---|---|---|---|---|
| D. | 12<br>− 5 | 9<br>− 2 | 16<br>− 9 | 12<br>− 4 | 16<br>− 7 | 9<br>− 3 | 17<br>− 8 |

| | | | | | | |
|---|---|---|---|---|---|---|
| E. | 12<br>− 2 | 14<br>− 7 | 13<br>− 8 | 12<br>− 6 | 8<br>− 7 | 11<br>− 6 | 13<br>− 7 |

| | | | | | | |
|---|---|---|---|---|---|---|
| F. | 10<br>− 8 | 7<br>− 4 | 10<br>− 5 | 12<br>− 9 | 14<br>− 9 | 7<br>− 6 | 10<br>− 7 |

| | | | | | | |
|---|---|---|---|---|---|---|
| G. | 7<br>− 2 | 14<br>− 6 | 11<br>− 8 | 6<br>− 1 | 10<br>− 4 | 17<br>− 9 | 15<br>− 7 |

| | | | | | | |
|---|---|---|---|---|---|---|
| H. | 15<br>− 6 | 8<br>− 2 | 12<br>− 8 | 4<br>− 2 | 11<br>− 2 | 5<br>− 3 | 8<br>− 4 |

## 2-, 3-, 4-, 5-, AND 6-DIGIT SUBTRACTION WITH REGROUPING

358 – 189

Subtract the ones.
You cannot subtract
9 from 8. Regroup 5 tens
as 4 tens and 10 ones.

```
    4 18
 3  5̶ 8̶
-1  8  9
       9
```

Subtract the tens.
You cannot subtract
8 tens from 4 tens.
Regroup 3 hundreds as 2
hundreds and 10 tens.

```
 2 14 18
 3̶ 5̶ 8̶
-1  8  9
    6  9
```

Subtract the hundreds.

```
 2 14 18
 3̶ 5̶ 8̶
-1  8  9
 1  6  9
```

**Solve each problem.**

A.
| 285 | 478 | 871 | 119 | 663 | 487 |
|---|---|---|---|---|---|
| − 167 | − 279 | − 557 | − 54 | − 49 | − 138 |

B.
| 852 | 579 | 265 | 565 | 726 | 419 |
|---|---|---|---|---|---|
| − 468 | − 498 | − 77 | − 178 | − 329 | − 287 |

C.
| 392 | 267 | 744 | 128 | 761 | 672 |
|---|---|---|---|---|---|
| − 263 | − 119 | − 498 | − 68 | − 332 | − 579 |

D.
| 9,311 | 5,322 | 9,435 | 4,254 | 2,414 | 4,592 |
|---|---|---|---|---|---|
| − 781 | − 693 | − 1,634 | − 2,965 | − 923 | − 1,497 |

E.
| 1,983 | 8,214 | 3,465 | 37,235 | 92,136 | 641,328 |
|---|---|---|---|---|---|
| − 1,288 | − 5,321 | − 2,877 | − 16,879 | − 48,657 | − 212,715 |

**MATH SUCCESS** RB-904108

# SUBTRACTION ACROSS ZEROS

2,001 − 148

Subtract the ones. You cannot take 8 from 1. You do not have enough ones, tens, or hundreds. Regroup from the thousands. 1,000 is 10 hundreds; 100 is 10 tens; 10 is 10 ones.

| Subtract the ones. | Subtract the tens. | Subtract the hundreds. | Subtract the thousands. |
|---|---|---|---|
| 2,001<br>− 148<br>**3** | 2,001<br>− 148<br>**53** | 2,001<br>− 148<br>**853** | 2,001<br>− 148<br>**1,853** |

## Solve each problem.

A.
| 500<br>− 324 | 7,000<br>− 4,968 | 300<br>− 136 | 4,001<br>− 1,292 | 8,000<br>− 4,449 | 2,000<br>− 376 |
|---|---|---|---|---|---|

B.
| 6,006<br>− 723 | 3,300<br>− 1,551 | 5,900<br>− 899 | 4,003<br>− 423 | 6,010<br>− 2,087 | 7,040<br>− 2,634 |
|---|---|---|---|---|---|

C.
| 80,700<br>− 2,859 | 58,000<br>− 1,846 | 36,000<br>− 3,582 | 95,000<br>− 7,432 | 89,000<br>− 14,832 | 45,000<br>− 16,548 |
|---|---|---|---|---|---|

D.
| 40,000<br>− 15,972 | 90,000<br>− 30,421 | 350,000<br>− 4,561 | 210,050<br>− 8,993 | 700,600<br>− 68,758 | 500,100<br>− 24,152 |
|---|---|---|---|---|---|

E.
| 400,000<br>− 27,764 | 800,000<br>− 28,828 | 100,000<br>− 9,999 | 200,000<br>− 7,147 | 700,000<br>− 28,282 | 600,000<br>− 66,666 |
|---|---|---|---|---|---|

## ADDITION AND SUBTRACTION PROBLEM SOLVING

**Use the information in the table to solve each problem.**

| City | Population in 2000 | Tallest Building | Height of Building |
|---|---|---|---|
| Boston | 589,141 | John Hancock Tower | 790 feet |
| Columbus | 711,470 | Rhodes State Office Tower | 629 feet |
| Denver | 554,445 | Republic Plaza | 714 feet |
| San Francisco | 776,773 | Transamerica Pyramid | 853 feet |

A.  How many more people lived in Boston than in Denver in 2000?

B.  What was the total population of Boston and Columbus in 2000?

C.  How many more people live in the two cities with the largest population than the two cities with the smallest population?

D.  How much taller is the Transamerica Pyramid than the John Hancock Tower?

E.  How much taller is the tallest building listed than the shortest one?

F.  If all four of the buildings in the data table were stacked on top of each other, how tall would the new structure be?

# ADDITION AND SUBTRACTION PROBLEM SOLVING

## Solve each problem.

A. The sixth graders of Jackson Elementary School want to read 1,000 books for their school's annual Read-A-Thon. So far, they have read 617 books. How many more books do they need to read to reach their goal?

_____

B. This year, the Jackson Elementary School goal for the Read-A-Thon is 7,000 books. The librarian told the students that they need to read 1,308 more books to reach their goal. How many books have the students read so far?

_____

C. Last year, the sixth graders read 682 books. The rest of the school read 5,972 books. The school missed their goal by 96 books. What was the school's goal last year?

_____

D. If the school increases its goal by 250 books each year, what will the school's goal be in 5 years if its goal this year is 7,000 books?

_____

E. Ms. Kay's class read 200 books. Mr. Bartle's class read 179 books. How many more books did Ms. Kay's class read than Mr. Bartle's class?

_____

F. National Children's Book Week takes place the third week of November. It was first held in 1919. How many years had it been celebrated by November 2002?

_____

# ADDITION AND SUBTRACTION ASSESSMENT

**Solve each problem.**

| | | | | |
|---|---|---|---|---|
| A. | 468<br>+ 382 | 168<br>+ 317 | 392<br>+ 62 | 4,735<br>+ 274 | 4,940<br>+ 4,801 |
| B. | 747<br>− 324 | 6,008<br>− 37 | 883<br>− 69 | 2,066<br>− 275 | 9,385<br>− 5,673 |
| C. | 1,872<br>+ 2,934 | 20,581<br>+ 4,664 | 26,863<br>+ 1,649 | 76,586<br>+ 35,708 | 64,749<br>+ 18,425 |
| D. | 8,604<br>− 7,238 | 5,657<br>− 3,948 | 9,400<br>− 2,848 | 4,006<br>− 2,378 | 6,300<br>− 4,677 |
| E. | 84,000<br>− 5,298 | 15,410<br>7,824<br>3,205<br>+ 5,138 | 28,000<br>− 6,243 | 8,738<br>21,465<br>98,109<br>+ 65,432 | 750,000<br>− 34,587 |

**Solve each problem.**

F. On Friday night, 37,589 people attended a concert. On Saturday, 48,122 attended. How many more people were at the Saturday night performance?

_____

How many people attended the two concerts combined?

_____

G. A large parking lot for an amusement park holds 2,000 vehicles. The parking attendant counted 219 empty spaces in the parking lot. How many vehicles are in the parking lot?

_____

**MATH SUCCESS** RB-904108

**Solve each problem.**

| | | | | | |
|---|---|---|---|---|---|
| A. | 208 <br> + 34 | 320 <br> + 413 | 6,855 <br> + 731 | 8,653 <br> + 272 | 4,684 <br> + 4,327 |
| B. | 678 <br> − 223 | 921 <br> − 68 | 840 <br> − 252 | 6,795 <br> − 486 | 7,428 <br> − 6,274 |
| C. | 12,975 <br> + 2,489 | 36,683 <br> + 1,024 | 84,315 <br> + 79,549 | 95,576 <br> + 13,142 | 54,700 <br> 23,405 <br> 43,617 <br> + 56,252 |
| D. | 9,242 <br> − 3,784 | 45,572 <br> − 9,784 | 42,510 <br> − 18,982 | 95,853 <br> − 61,963 | 400,000 <br> − 24,351 |
| E. | 4,921 <br> + 138 | 8,480 <br> + 1,842 | 24,426 <br> + 3,557 | 7,221 <br> − 5,321 | 18,347 <br> − 11,358 |

**Solve each problem.**

F. The Cool Kid Computer Company produced 50,237 computer games during the first half of the year and 65,710 computer games during the last half of the year. How many more games did it produce during the last half of the year?

How many computer games did it produce during the entire year?

G. Greg kept a record of the number of visits to his Web site during the month of February. The first week, he had 1,187 visits. The second week, he had 745 visits. The third week, he had 2,132 visits, and the fourth week, he had 3,521 visits. How many total visits did he have in February?

# MULTIPLICATION FACTS REVIEW

**Solve each problem.**

A.
$\begin{array}{r} 6 \\ \times 4 \\ \hline \end{array}$
$\begin{array}{r} 3 \\ \times 1 \\ \hline \end{array}$
$\begin{array}{r} 9 \\ \times 7 \\ \hline \end{array}$
$\begin{array}{r} 8 \\ \times 3 \\ \hline \end{array}$
$\begin{array}{r} 7 \\ \times 7 \\ \hline \end{array}$
$\begin{array}{r} 5 \\ \times 8 \\ \hline \end{array}$
$\begin{array}{r} 6 \\ \times 7 \\ \hline \end{array}$

B.
$\begin{array}{r} 2 \\ \times 3 \\ \hline \end{array}$
$\begin{array}{r} 6 \\ \times 9 \\ \hline \end{array}$
$\begin{array}{r} 5 \\ \times 4 \\ \hline \end{array}$
$\begin{array}{r} 4 \\ \times 9 \\ \hline \end{array}$
$\begin{array}{r} 6 \\ \times 6 \\ \hline \end{array}$
$\begin{array}{r} 9 \\ \times 8 \\ \hline \end{array}$
$\begin{array}{r} 5 \\ \times 9 \\ \hline \end{array}$

C.
$\begin{array}{r} 8 \\ \times 8 \\ \hline \end{array}$
$\begin{array}{r} 2 \\ \times 5 \\ \hline \end{array}$
$\begin{array}{r} 1 \\ \times 4 \\ \hline \end{array}$
$\begin{array}{r} 4 \\ \times 6 \\ \hline \end{array}$
$\begin{array}{r} 9 \\ \times 5 \\ \hline \end{array}$
$\begin{array}{r} 3 \\ \times 7 \\ \hline \end{array}$
$\begin{array}{r} 8 \\ \times 6 \\ \hline \end{array}$

D.
$\begin{array}{r} 4 \\ \times 7 \\ \hline \end{array}$
$\begin{array}{r} 7 \\ \times 5 \\ \hline \end{array}$
$\begin{array}{r} 2 \\ \times 2 \\ \hline \end{array}$
$\begin{array}{r} 5 \\ \times 1 \\ \hline \end{array}$
$\begin{array}{r} 7 \\ \times 4 \\ \hline \end{array}$
$\begin{array}{r} 8 \\ \times 9 \\ \hline \end{array}$
$\begin{array}{r} 6 \\ \times 3 \\ \hline \end{array}$

E.
$\begin{array}{r} 8 \\ \times 7 \\ \hline \end{array}$
$\begin{array}{r} 4 \\ \times 3 \\ \hline \end{array}$
$\begin{array}{r} 5 \\ \times 5 \\ \hline \end{array}$
$\begin{array}{r} 4 \\ \times 2 \\ \hline \end{array}$
$\begin{array}{r} 9 \\ \times 6 \\ \hline \end{array}$
$\begin{array}{r} 4 \\ \times 8 \\ \hline \end{array}$
$\begin{array}{r} 3 \\ \times 5 \\ \hline \end{array}$

F.
$\begin{array}{r} 9 \\ \times 9 \\ \hline \end{array}$
$\begin{array}{r} 1 \\ \times 6 \\ \hline \end{array}$
$\begin{array}{r} 7 \\ \times 9 \\ \hline \end{array}$
$\begin{array}{r} 6 \\ \times 5 \\ \hline \end{array}$
$\begin{array}{r} 2 \\ \times 7 \\ \hline \end{array}$
$\begin{array}{r} 7 \\ \times 1 \\ \hline \end{array}$
$\begin{array}{r} 9 \\ \times 4 \\ \hline \end{array}$

G.
$\begin{array}{r} 5 \\ \times 6 \\ \hline \end{array}$
$\begin{array}{r} 8 \\ \times 4 \\ \hline \end{array}$
$\begin{array}{r} 5 \\ \times 7 \\ \hline \end{array}$
$\begin{array}{r} 8 \\ \times 2 \\ \hline \end{array}$
$\begin{array}{r} 3 \\ \times 3 \\ \hline \end{array}$
$\begin{array}{r} 6 \\ \times 2 \\ \hline \end{array}$
$\begin{array}{r} 1 \\ \times 8 \\ \hline \end{array}$

H.
$\begin{array}{r} 9 \\ \times 1 \\ \hline \end{array}$
$\begin{array}{r} 6 \\ \times 8 \\ \hline \end{array}$
$\begin{array}{r} 3 \\ \times 9 \\ \hline \end{array}$
$\begin{array}{r} 7 \\ \times 8 \\ \hline \end{array}$
$\begin{array}{r} 4 \\ \times 4 \\ \hline \end{array}$
$\begin{array}{r} 8 \\ \times 5 \\ \hline \end{array}$
$\begin{array}{r} 2 \\ \times 9 \\ \hline \end{array}$

**MATH SUCCESS** RB-904108 © Rainbow Bridge Publishing

## 2-, 3-, 4-, AND 5-DIGIT BY 1-DIGIT MULTIPLICATION

783 x 6

| Multiply 6 ones by 3 ones. Regroup 18 ones as 1 ten, 8 ones. | Multiply 6 ones by 8 tens. Add the regrouped ten. Regroup 49 tens as 4 hundreds, 9 tens. | Multiply 6 ones by 7 hundreds. Add the 4 regrouped hundreds. |
|---|---|---|
| ₁<br>7 8 **3**<br>x   **6**<br>    **8** | ₄ ₁<br>7 **8** 3<br>x   **6**<br>  **9** 8 | ₄ ₁<br>**7** 8 3<br>x   **6**<br>**4 , 6** 9 8 |

**Solve each problem.**

A.
$$85 \times 5 \qquad 45 \times 8 \qquad 58 \times 2 \qquad 49 \times 3 \qquad 62 \times 7$$

B.
$$509 \times 9 \qquad 211 \times 4 \qquad 336 \times 5 \qquad 933 \times 6 \qquad 835 \times 3$$

C.
$$362 \times 8 \qquad 841 \times 5 \qquad 537 \times 3 \qquad 719 \times 6 \qquad 631 \times 9$$

D.
$$3{,}675 \times 6 \qquad 5{,}810 \times 9 \qquad 4{,}861 \times 5 \qquad 9{,}283 \times 3 \qquad 8{,}614 \times 7$$

E.
$$27{,}524 \times 5 \qquad 85{,}412 \times 3 \qquad 39{,}567 \times 6 \qquad 48{,}418 \times 4 \qquad 75{,}629 \times 8$$

## 2-, 3-, AND 4-DIGIT BY 2-DIGIT MULTIPLICATION

75 x 52

| Multiply the top number by the ones digit of the bottom number. Regroup if necessary. | Put a zero in the ones column as a placeholder. Multiply the top number by the tens digit of the bottom number. Regroup if necessary. | Add. |
|---|---|---|
| ¹<br>**7 5**<br>x 5 **2**<br>**1 5 0** | ²<br>**7 5**<br>x **5** 2<br>1 5 0<br>**3 , 7 5 0** | **7 5**<br>x 5 2<br>1 5 0<br>+ 3 , 7 5 0<br>**3 , 9 0 0** |

**Solve each problem.**

A.
| 25 | 32 | 24 | 61 | 78 |
|---|---|---|---|---|
| x 74 | x 59 | x 96 | x 56 | x 14 |

B.
| 48 | 86 | 62 | 78 | 95 |
|---|---|---|---|---|
| x 44 | x 57 | x 96 | x 36 | x 34 |

C.
| 953 | 444 | 872 | 709 | 414 |
|---|---|---|---|---|
| x 25 | x 38 | x 19 | x 56 | x 41 |

D.
| 779 | 982 | 486 | 695 | 728 |
|---|---|---|---|---|
| x 98 | x 63 | x 72 | x 89 | x 56 |

E.
| 5,261 | 5,086 | 2,158 | 6,572 | 6,321 |
|---|---|---|---|---|
| x 39 | x 57 | x 73 | x 94 | x 62 |

## 3- AND 4-DIGIT BY 3-DIGIT MULTIPLICATION

872 x 494

**Multiply the top number by the ones digit of the bottom number. Regroup if necessary.**

```
    2
  8 7 2
x   4 9 4
3 , 4 8 8
```

**Put a 0 in the ones column as a placeholder. Multiply the top number by the tens digit of the bottom number. Regroup if necessary.**

```
    6 1
  8 7 2
x   4 9 4
3 , 4 8 8
7 8 , 4 8 0
```

**Put 0s in the ones and tens columns as placeholders. Multiply the top number by the hundreds digit of the bottom number. Regroup if necessary.**

```
      2
    8 7 2
x     4 9 4
  3 , 4 8 8
  7 8 , 4 8 0
+ 3 4 8 , 8 0 0
```

**Add.**

```
      8 7 2
x     4 9 4
  3 , 4 8 8
  7 8 , 4 8 0
+ 3 4 8 , 8 0 0
  4 3 0 , 7 6 8
```

**Solve each problem.**

A.
```
  762        503        638        982        594
x 381      x 741      x 897      x 872      x 439
```

B.
```
  287        758        165        284        477
x 287      x 439      x 825      x 833      x 360
```

C.
```
4,610      3,944      2,775      1,615      2,138
x  239     x  307     x  173     x  239     x  256
```

# DIVISION FACTS REVIEW

**Solve each problem.**

A.  $1\overline{)9}$  $6\overline{)30}$  $9\overline{)81}$  $7\overline{)56}$  $4\overline{)24}$  $8\overline{)64}$  $3\overline{)6}$

B.  $8\overline{)48}$  $4\overline{)32}$  $6\overline{)6}$  $3\overline{)12}$  $5\overline{)35}$  $1\overline{)3}$  $9\overline{)54}$

C.  $9\overline{)27}$  $7\overline{)35}$  $9\overline{)63}$  $5\overline{)25}$  $2\overline{)4}$  $7\overline{)63}$  $4\overline{)20}$

D.  $8\overline{)56}$  $2\overline{)16}$  $5\overline{)30}$  $2\overline{)8}$  $1\overline{)5}$  $6\overline{)24}$  $9\overline{)36}$

E.  $4\overline{)16}$  $3\overline{)9}$  $7\overline{)14}$  $6\overline{)54}$  $4\overline{)28}$  $5\overline{)45}$  $6\overline{)36}$

F.  $5\overline{)40}$  $2\overline{)12}$  $1\overline{)7}$  $8\overline{)32}$  $9\overline{)72}$  $7\overline{)21}$  $8\overline{)72}$

G.  $9\overline{)18}$  $8\overline{)8}$  $4\overline{)36}$  $5\overline{)15}$  $3\overline{)18}$  $6\overline{)48}$  $9\overline{)45}$

H.  $7\overline{)28}$  $5\overline{)10}$  $3\overline{)24}$  $7\overline{)49}$  $4\overline{)4}$  $8\overline{)40}$  $7\overline{)42}$

# 3- AND 4-DIGIT BY 1-DIGIT DIVISION

3)1,585

**Think:** 3)15
3 goes into 1 zero times.
3 goes into 15 five times.

Divide.
Multiply 5 x 3.
Subtract 15 – 15.
Bring down the 8 tens.

```
      5
3)1,585
 -1 5↓
    08
```

**Think:** 3)8
3 goes into 8 two times.

Divide.
Multiply 2 x 3.
Subtract 8 – 6.
Bring down the 5 ones.

```
     52
3)1,585
 -15 |
   08|
   - 6↓
     25
```

**Think:** 3)25
3 goes into 25 eight times.

Divide.
Multiply 3 x 8.
Subtract 25 – 24.
Compare 1 < 3.
Write the difference as
the remainder.

```
    528 r1
3)1,585
 -15
   08
   - 6
     25
   - 24
      1
```

**Solve each problem.**

A.  7)126        5)190        4)864        6)306        8)128

B.  3)643        4)857        6)674        5)569        3)605

C.  7)1,481      6)1,624      5)4,566      4)2,050      8)5,666

## 3-, 4-, AND 5-DIGIT BY 2-DIGIT DIVISION

$32\overline{)7,980}$

**Think:** $32\overline{)79}$
32 goes into 7 zero times.
32 goes into 79 two times.

Divide.
Multiply 2 x 32.
Subtract 79 – 64.
Bring down the 8 tens.

```
      2
32)7,980
  -6 4↓
   1 5 8
```

**Think:** $32\overline{)158}$
32 goes into 158
four times.

Divide.
Multiply 4 x 32.
Subtract 158 – 128.
Bring down the 0 ones.

```
     24
32)7,980
  -6 4
   1 5 8
  -1 2 8↓
     3 0 0
```

**Think:** $32\overline{)300}$
32 goes into 300
nine times.

Divide.
Multiply 9 x 32.
Subtract 300 – 288.
Compare 12 < 32.
Write the difference as
the remainder.

```
     249 r12
32)7,980
  -6 4
   1 5 8
  -1 2 8
     3 0 0
    -2 8 8
       1 2
```

## Solve each problem.

A. $46\overline{)857}$      $28\overline{)635}$      $32\overline{)8,329}$      $55\overline{)1,728}$

B. $21\overline{)4,670}$      $17\overline{)4,287}$      $58\overline{)2,439}$      $73\overline{)8,967}$

C. $91\overline{)8,743}$      $52\overline{)2,647}$      $37\overline{)86,322}$      $48\overline{)97,243}$

**MATH SUCCESS** RB-904108      © Rainbow Bridge Publishing

## 4-, 5-, AND 6-DIGIT BY 3-DIGIT DIVISION

$397\overline{)23,925}$

With large numbers, it may be helpful to estimate.

**Estimate:** $400\overline{)2,400}$
400 goes into 2 zero times.
400 goes into 24 zero times.
400 goes into 2,400 six times.

Divide.
Multiply 6 x 397.
Subtract 2,392 – 2,382.
Bring down the 5 ones.

$$\begin{array}{r} 6 \\ 397\overline{)23,925} \\ -2382\downarrow \\ \hline 105 \end{array}$$

**Think:** $397\overline{)105}$
397 goes into 105 zero times.

Divide.
Multiply 0 x 397.
Subtract 105 – 0.
Compare 105 < 397.
Write the difference as the remainder.

$$\begin{array}{r} 60\ r105 \\ 397\overline{)23,925} \\ -2382 \\ \hline 105 \\ -\ \ 0 \\ \hline 105 \end{array}$$

**Solve each problem.**

A.  $845\overline{)5,070}$       $405\overline{)3,240}$       $624\overline{)4,368}$       $832\overline{)3,736}$

B.  $123\overline{)8,711}$       $537\overline{)3,765}$       $189\overline{)6,498}$       $273\overline{)74,618}$

C.  $213\overline{)65,827}$       $181\overline{)90,699}$       $289\overline{)79,346}$       $964\overline{)385,678}$

# MULTIPLICATION AND DIVISION PROBLEM SOLVING

## Use the information to solve each problem.

A roller coaster ride at the Fun-For-All Amusement Park usually operates 4 cars, each of which carries 32 people. During the park's peak hours, 1,250 people wait in line to ride the roller coaster. The ride takes 4 minutes, which includes loading and unloading passengers.

A. How many people can be on the ride at one time if all 4 cars are running?

_____

B. If all 4 cars are running, how many times would each car have to run so that all 1,250 people could take a ride?

_____

C. About how long would it take for all 1,250 people in line to have a ride if all 4 cars are running? (Hint: Use your answer from problem B.)

_____

D. If the ride ran 5 cars instead of 4, about how much less time would it take for all 1,250 people to have a ride? (Hint: Repeat the process that you used to solve problem C.)

_____

E. The park is open for 9 hours each day. If the roller coaster operates continuously from opening to closing, how many times will each car run in a day?

_____

F. The roller coaster closes for maintenance for 48 minutes. How many potential riders cannot ride the roller coaster that day?

_____

**MATH SUCCESS** RB-904108

# MULTIPLICATION AND DIVISION PROBLEM SOLVING

**Solve each problem.**

A. The Perfectly Popped Popcorn Company did a study and found that the average popcorn consumer eats about 65 quarts of popcorn per year. If you eat this much, how many quarts of popcorn will you have consumed in 20 years?

_____

B. How long will it take a person to consume 585 quarts of popcorn if he eats 65 quarts per year?

_____

C. Perfectly Popped sells a variety of popcorn flavors in large, decorated tubs. If Jenna orders 36 matching tubs containing 216 gallons of popcorn in all, how much popcorn is in each tub?

_____

D. The staff at a theater snack counter has found that 32 ounces of popcorn kernels make enough popcorn to fill 20 small bags. How many small bags could they fill with 18 pounds of popcorn? (Hint: There are 16 ounces in 1 pound.)

_____

E. The cargo trucks that distribute the packaged popcorn to retailers hold 95 tubs of popcorn each. How many trucks will it take to distribute 1,250 tubs of popcorn?

_____

F. Perfectly Popped received a shipment of 227 boxes of popcorn kernels. These were divided into 8 groups. Each group contained 28 boxes except one. How many boxes were in that group?

_____

# MULTIPLICATION AND DIVISION ASSESSMENT

**Solve each problem.**

A.
$$\begin{array}{r} 79 \\ \times\ 7 \\ \hline \end{array}$$
$$\begin{array}{r} 341 \\ \times\ 5 \\ \hline \end{array}$$
$$\begin{array}{r} 147 \\ \times\ 2 \\ \hline \end{array}$$
$$\begin{array}{r} 247 \\ \times\ 59 \\ \hline \end{array}$$
$$\begin{array}{r} 2,099 \\ \times\ 6 \\ \hline \end{array}$$

B.
$$\begin{array}{r} 402 \\ \times\ 88 \\ \hline \end{array}$$
$$\begin{array}{r} 947 \\ \times\ 163 \\ \hline \end{array}$$
$$\begin{array}{r} 1,637 \\ \times\ 22 \\ \hline \end{array}$$
$$\begin{array}{r} 8,600 \\ \times\ 82 \\ \hline \end{array}$$
$$\begin{array}{r} 5,704 \\ \times\ 822 \\ \hline \end{array}$$

**Solve each problem.**

C. $7\overline{)63}$ $3\overline{)48}$ $6\overline{)546}$ $6\overline{)8,514}$

D. $62\overline{)4,263}$ $32\overline{)6,744}$ $701\overline{)40,008}$ $165\overline{)67,042}$

**Solve each problem.**

E. Doug has been training to run in a marathon. He ran 63 miles each week for the past year (52 weeks). How many miles did Doug run altogether?

F. Kendra is knitting some blankets to sell at a craft fair. She has 215 feet of trim, and she needs 23 feet for each blanket. How many blankets can she make?

How much trim will she have left over?

**MATH SUCCESS** RB-904108          © Rainbow Bridge Publishing

**Solve each problem.**

A.
$$37 \times 4$$
$$415 \times 6$$
$$542 \times 81$$
$$427 \times 22$$

B.
$$4{,}804 \times 7$$
$$647 \times 142$$
$$6{,}521 \times 34$$
$$1{,}254 \times 89$$

**Solve each problem.**

C. $9\overline{)81}$  $9\overline{)828}$  $4\overline{)39}$  $8\overline{)965}$

D. $5\overline{)4{,}517}$  $17\overline{)60}$  $17\overline{)520}$  $189\overline{)16{,}350}$

**Solve each problem.**

E. Susan owns a chain of dress shops. Last month, she sold 1,432 dresses. Each dress sold for an average of $65.00. About how much money did Susan make from selling the dresses?

_____

F. Mitchell has collected 1,327 marbles. He has divided the marbles equally into 12 jars.

How many marbles are in each jar?

_____

How many marbles are leftover?

_____

# WRITING FRACTIONS ON A NUMBER LINE

You can represent fractions on a number line. If an interval from 0 to 1 is divided into 6 equal pieces, the length of any one of the pieces represents $\frac{1}{6}$.
The fraction $\frac{1}{6}$ can also be thought of as $1 \div 6$ since the interval is divided into 6 equal parts.

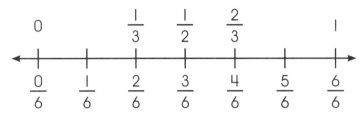

**Write the missing fractions on each number line.**

A.

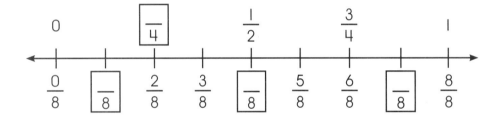

B.

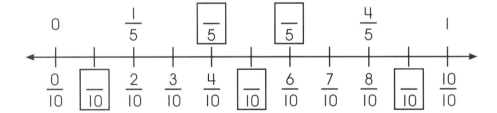

C.

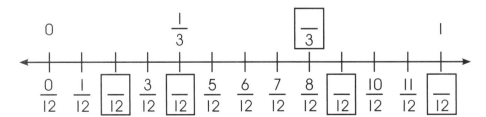

# EQUIVALENT FRACTIONS

If a numerator and a denominator are either multiplied or divided by the same number, then the new fraction is equivalent (or equal to) the original fraction.

$$\frac{4}{6} = \frac{4 \times 2}{6 \times 2} = \frac{8}{12}$$

$$\frac{4}{6} = \frac{4 \times 3}{6 \times 3} = \frac{12}{18}$$

$$\frac{4}{6} = \frac{4 \div 2}{6 \div 2} = \frac{2}{3}$$

So, $\frac{4}{6}$, $\frac{8}{12}$, $\frac{12}{18}$, and $\frac{2}{3}$ are all equivalent fractions.

**Write two equivalent fractions for each fraction.**

A.    $\frac{2}{4} =$    $=$      $\frac{2}{12} =$    $=$      $\frac{8}{14} =$    $=$      $\frac{4}{18} =$    $=$

B.    $\frac{10}{24} =$    $=$      $\frac{4}{9} =$    $=$      $\frac{10}{20} =$    $=$      $\frac{18}{24} =$    $=$

C.    $\frac{2}{16} =$    $=$      $\frac{10}{12} =$    $=$      $\frac{8}{9} =$    $=$      $\frac{4}{10} =$    $=$

D.    $\frac{3}{24} =$    $=$      $\frac{3}{10} =$    $=$      $\frac{7}{18} =$    $=$      $\frac{18}{40} =$    $=$

**Complete each equivalent fraction.**

E.    $\frac{1}{11} = \frac{}{33}$      $\frac{1}{4} = \frac{}{20}$      $\frac{4}{16} = \frac{}{32}$      $\frac{8}{9} = \frac{}{54}$

F.    $\frac{3}{15} = \frac{}{45}$      $\frac{2}{6} = \frac{}{36}$      $\frac{5}{16} = \frac{}{48}$      $\frac{3}{8} = \frac{}{24}$

G.    $\frac{3}{18} = \frac{}{36}$      $\frac{12}{18} = \frac{}{54}$      $\frac{1}{30} = \frac{3}{}$      $\frac{2}{11} = \frac{}{33}$

H.    $\frac{7}{11} = \frac{42}{}$      $\frac{4}{10} = \frac{}{50}$      $\frac{10}{40} = \frac{30}{}$      $\frac{5}{7} = \frac{}{49}$

# GREATEST COMMON FACTORS

A **factor** is a number that another number can be evenly divided by. The greatest common factor (GCF) is the greatest factor that two or more numbers have in common.

To find the greatest common factor, write the factors of each number. Circle the common factors. Then, write the GCF.

Find the GCF of 12 and 18.

Factors of 12: (1) (2) (3) 4, (6) 12

Factors of 18: (1) (2) (3) (6) 9, 18          **GCF = 6**

**Find the greatest common factor (GCF) of each pair of numbers.**

A.      6
        18
        GCF:

B.      15
        20
        GCF:

C.      24
        32
        GCF:

D.      14
        21
        GCF:

E.      14
        35
        GCF:

F.      9
        15
        GCF:

G.      18
        27
        GCF:

H.      4
        12
        GCF:

I.      15
        40
        GCF:

J.      9
        12
        GCF:

K.      7
        21
        GCF:

L.      15
        35
        GCF:

## SIMPLEST FORM

Write the fraction $\frac{42}{56}$ in simplest form.

Find the GCF of the numerator and denominator.

42: (1,) (2,) 3, 6, (7,) (14,) 21, 42

56: (1,) (2,) 4, (7,) 8, (14,) 28, 56

**GCF = 14**

Divide the numerator and the denominator by the GCF.

$$\frac{42}{56} \div \frac{14}{14} = \frac{3}{4}$$

**Write each fraction in simplest form.**

A. $\frac{4}{6} =$      $\frac{5}{10} =$      $\frac{9}{15} =$      $\frac{8}{14} =$      $\frac{3}{15} =$

B. $\frac{3}{27} =$      $\frac{6}{18} =$      $\frac{15}{18} =$      $\frac{28}{30} =$      $\frac{5}{20} =$

C. $\frac{6}{21} =$      $\frac{28}{42} =$      $\frac{22}{30} =$      $\frac{16}{32} =$      $\frac{35}{50} =$

D. $\frac{7}{21} =$      $\frac{19}{38} =$      $\frac{48}{60} =$      $\frac{10}{20} =$      $\frac{22}{32} =$

E. $\frac{34}{68} =$      $\frac{22}{88} =$      $\frac{26}{28} =$      $\frac{18}{90} =$      $\frac{75}{80} =$

## LEAST COMMON MULTIPLES

The **least common multiple (LCM)** is the smallest number that is a multiple of two or more numbers.

To find the least common multiple, write the first few multiples of each number. Write the LCM.

Find the LCM of 6 and 8.

Multiples of 6: 6, 12, 18, (24,) 30, 36, 42, 48

Multiples of 8: 8, 16, (24,) 32, 40, 48          **LCM = 24**

**Find the least common multiple (LCM) of each pair of numbers.**

A.　　6
　　　2
　　LCM:

B.　　4
　　　8
　　LCM:

C.　　5
　　　3
　　LCM:

D.　　4
　　　6
　　LCM:

E.　　8
　　　12
　　LCM:

F.　　6
　　　10
　　LCM:

**Find the least common multiple (LCM) of each set of numbers.**

G.　　6
　　　5
　　　15
　　LCM:

H.　　4
　　　9
　　　18
　　LCM:

I.　　8
　　　10
　　　20
　　LCM:

J.　　10
　　　15
　　　30
　　LCM:

**MATH SUCCESS** RB-904108　　　　© Rainbow Bridge Publishing

# LEAST COMMON DENOMINATORS

The **least common denominator (LCD)** of two fractions is the least common multiple of their denominators. Two fractions have a common denominator if their denominators are the same. To find the least common denominator, write the multiples of each denominator. Circle the common multiples. Write the least common denominator.

Find the LCD of $\dfrac{5}{8}$ and $\dfrac{7}{12}$ .

Multiples of 8: 8, 16, ⟨24⟩

Multiples of 12: 12, ⟨24⟩

**LCD = 24**

Write each equivalent fraction with the common denominator of 24.

$$\frac{5}{8} = \frac{}{24} \qquad\qquad \frac{7}{12} = \frac{}{24}$$

$$\frac{5}{8} \times \frac{3}{3} = \frac{15}{24} \qquad\qquad \frac{7}{12} \times \frac{2}{2} = \frac{14}{24}$$

**Rewrite each pair of fractions using the least common denominator (LCD).**

A.  $\dfrac{1}{9}$ and $\dfrac{1}{3}$  $\qquad$ $\dfrac{1}{3}$ and $\dfrac{1}{6}$  $\qquad$ $\dfrac{5}{6}$ and $\dfrac{2}{5}$

B.  $\dfrac{3}{8}$ and $\dfrac{2}{3}$  $\qquad$ $\dfrac{1}{3}$ and $\dfrac{4}{9}$  $\qquad$ $\dfrac{4}{5}$ and $\dfrac{5}{9}$

C.  $\dfrac{2}{4}$ and $\dfrac{3}{7}$  $\qquad$ $\dfrac{2}{3}$ and $\dfrac{7}{8}$  $\qquad$ $\dfrac{3}{5}$ and $\dfrac{5}{6}$

D.  $\dfrac{1}{8}$ and $\dfrac{1}{16}$  $\qquad$ $\dfrac{1}{12}$ and $\dfrac{1}{4}$  $\qquad$ $\dfrac{1}{18}$ and $\dfrac{1}{9}$

E.  $\dfrac{1}{4}$ and $\dfrac{5}{18}$  $\qquad$ $\dfrac{3}{7}$ and $\dfrac{3}{8}$  $\qquad$ $\dfrac{1}{2}$ and $\dfrac{4}{11}$

# COMPARING AND ORDERING FRACTIONS

To compare fractions, the fractions need to have common denominators.

Compare $\frac{7}{9}$ and $\frac{5}{7}$.

| Find the LCD. | Write equivalent fractions with the LCD. | Compare the numerators. |
|---|---|---|
| 7: 7, 14, 21, 28, 35, 42, 49, 56, (63) | $\frac{7}{9} = \frac{49}{63}$ | $\frac{49}{63}$ > $\frac{45}{63}$ |
| 9: 9, 18, 27, 36, 45, 54, (63) | $\frac{5}{7} = \frac{45}{63}$ | So, $\frac{7}{9}$ > $\frac{5}{7}$ . |
| **LCD = 63** | | |

**Write >, <, or = to compare each pair of fractions.**

A.  $\frac{3}{6} \square \frac{4}{8}$      $\frac{4}{5} \square \frac{10}{15}$      $\frac{3}{5} \square \frac{1}{2}$      $\frac{2}{7} \square \frac{1}{3}$

B.  $\frac{2}{3} \square \frac{5}{8}$      $\frac{1}{3} \square \frac{2}{5}$      $\frac{1}{8} \square \frac{1}{16}$      $\frac{5}{9} \square \frac{4}{8}$

**Write each set of fractions in order from least to greatest.**

C.  $\frac{1}{3}$ , $\frac{7}{12}$ , $\frac{5}{6}$          $\frac{3}{4}$ , $\frac{7}{8}$ , $\frac{13}{16}$          $\frac{3}{4}$ , $\frac{5}{7}$ , $\frac{9}{14}$

D.  $\frac{5}{6}$ , $\frac{3}{4}$ , $\frac{1}{2}$          $\frac{3}{4}$ , $\frac{3}{5}$ , $\frac{3}{8}$          $\frac{4}{5}$ , $\frac{17}{20}$ , $\frac{3}{4}$

**MATH SUCCESS** RB-904108                    © Rainbow Bridge Publishing

# FRACTIONS PROBLEM SOLVING

**Solve each problem. Simplify if possible.**

A. A medium pizza was cut into 10 equal slices. Eight slices of pizza were eaten. Write a fraction to show how much pizza was eaten.

_____

B. An extra large pepperoni pizza was cut into 16 equal slices. A total of 10 slices of pizza were eaten. What fraction of the pizza was left over?

_____

C. The school cafeteria orders pizza every Friday from a local restaurant. About $\frac{2}{3}$ of the students who eat pizza for lunch prefer pepperoni. If the school orders 48 pizzas altogether, how many of these should be pepperoni?

_____

D. In a survey about vegetable toppings, $\frac{3}{4}$ of the sixth-grade students said that they liked green peppers on their pizza, $\frac{5}{8}$ said that they liked mushrooms, and $\frac{2}{3}$ of the students said that they liked onions. (Some students liked more than one choice.) Which of the three choices do the greatest number of students like?

_____

Which of the three choices do the fewest number of students like?

_____

# FRACTIONS PROBLEM SOLVING

**Use the bar graph to solve each problem. Simplify if possible.**

The Chamber of Commerce surveyed tourists to see which activities they participated in while visiting the capital city. The graph shows the fraction of all tourists who took part in each activity.

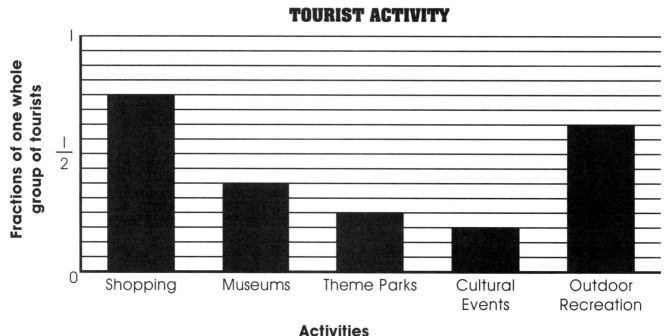

**TOURIST ACTIVITY**

A. Which activities were chosen by more than $\frac{1}{2}$ of the tourists? _____

_____

B. What fraction of the tourists participated in the least popular activity? _____

C. What fraction of the tourists participated in the most popular activity? _____

D. Which activity did $\frac{5}{8}$ of the tourists participate in? _____

E. What fraction of the tourists visited theme parks? _____

F. Which activity did tourists participate in half as much as shopping? _____

G. Which activity did $\frac{1}{4}$ of the tourists participate in? _____

**MATH SUCCESS** RB-904108

**Write each missing fraction on the number line.**

A.
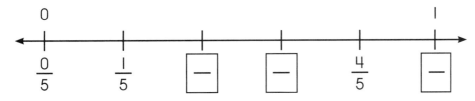

**Circle all of the fractions that are equal to $\frac{9}{12}$.**

B.  $\frac{12}{16}$        $\frac{3}{4}$        $\frac{2}{3}$        $\frac{21}{28}$        $\frac{30}{40}$        $\frac{24}{36}$

**Find the greatest common factor (GCF) for each pair of numbers.**

C.  44, 33            28, 35            48, 36            20, 50

**Write each fraction in simplest form.**

D.  $\frac{6}{9} =$            $\frac{18}{60} =$            $\frac{12}{54} =$

**Find the least common multiple (LCM) for each pair of numbers.**

E.  10, 20            18, 36            12, 18            3, 5

**Find the least common denominator (LCD) for each pair of fractions.**

F.  $\frac{1}{4}$ and $\frac{4}{8}$        $\frac{2}{3}$ and $\frac{4}{5}$        $\frac{3}{12}$ and $\frac{6}{8}$        $\frac{4}{10}$ and $\frac{6}{15}$

   LCD: _____        LCD: _____        LCD: _____        LCD: _____

**Write >, <, or = to compare each pair of fractions.**

G.  $\frac{2}{3}$ ☐ $\frac{3}{5}$        $\frac{5}{12}$ ☐ $\frac{1}{3}$        $\frac{7}{10}$ ☐ $\frac{5}{9}$

**Write each missing fraction on the number line.**

A.

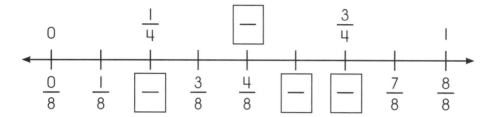

$$0 \qquad \frac{1}{4} \qquad \boxed{\phantom{-}} \qquad \frac{3}{4} \qquad 1$$

$$\frac{0}{8} \qquad \frac{1}{8} \qquad \boxed{\phantom{-}} \qquad \frac{3}{8} \qquad \frac{4}{8} \qquad \boxed{\phantom{-}} \qquad \boxed{\phantom{-}} \qquad \frac{7}{8} \qquad \frac{8}{8}$$

**Circle all of the fractions that are equal to $\frac{6}{16}$ .**

B. $\quad \frac{3}{8} \qquad\qquad \frac{1}{3} \qquad\qquad \frac{9}{24} \qquad\qquad \frac{6}{24} \qquad\qquad \frac{12}{32} \qquad\qquad \frac{18}{36}$

**Find the greatest common factor (GCF) for each pair of numbers.**

C. $\quad$ 40, 15 $\qquad\qquad$ 15, 35 $\qquad\qquad$ 12, 30 $\qquad\qquad$ 40, 60

**Write each fraction in simplest form.**

D. $\qquad \frac{6}{8} = \qquad\qquad\qquad \frac{14}{16} = \qquad\qquad\qquad \frac{25}{75} =$

**Find the least common multiple (LCM) for each pair of numbers.**

E. $\quad$ 20, 30 $\qquad\qquad$ 12, 20 $\qquad\qquad$ 4, 14 $\qquad\qquad$ 5, 7

**Find the least common denominator (LCD) for each pair of fractions.**

F. $\quad \frac{1}{3}$ and $\frac{7}{9}$ $\qquad\qquad \frac{3}{5}$ and $\frac{2}{4}$ $\qquad\qquad \frac{4}{10}$ and $\frac{3}{4}$

$\quad$ LCD: _____ $\qquad\qquad$ LCD: _____ $\qquad\qquad$ LCD: _____

**Write >, <, or = to compare each pair of fractions.**

G. $\quad \frac{3}{4} \ \square \ \frac{7}{10} \qquad\qquad \frac{6}{8} \ \square \ \frac{7}{9} \qquad\qquad \frac{11}{15} \ \square \ \frac{21}{30}$

**MATH SUCCESS** RB-904108 $\qquad\qquad\qquad$ © Rainbow Bridge Publishing

# WRITING MIXED NUMBERS

A **mixed number** is made up of a whole number and a fraction. A mixed number is a number greater than 1 that is between two whole numbers.

$$\text{whole number} \longrightarrow 3\frac{1}{2} \longleftarrow \text{fraction}$$

An **improper fraction** has a numerator that is greater than or equal to the denominator. An improper fraction is greater than or equal to 1. An improper fraction can be written as a mixed number.

$$\text{improper fraction} \longrightarrow \frac{7}{2} = 3\frac{1}{2} \longleftarrow \text{mixed number}$$

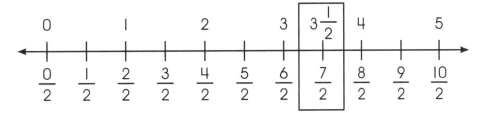

Write $\frac{10}{4}$ as a mixed number.

The fraction bar can be read as "divided by." So, $\frac{10}{4}$ means "10 divided by 4."

**Think:** How many times does 4 go into 10?
Four goes into ten 2 times, with 2 remaining.

So, $\frac{10}{4} = 2\frac{2}{4} = 2\frac{1}{2}$

$$\begin{array}{r} 2 \leftarrow \textbf{number of wholes} \\ 4\overline{)10} \\ -8 \\ \hline 2 \leftarrow \textbf{number of fourths remaining} \end{array}$$

**Write each improper fraction as a whole number or a mixed number. Simplify if possible.**

A.  $\dfrac{4}{3} =$  $\qquad$  $\dfrac{5}{2} =$  $\qquad$  $\dfrac{25}{5} =$  $\qquad$  $\dfrac{17}{12} =$  $\qquad$  $\dfrac{26}{3} =$

B.  $\dfrac{10}{3} =$  $\qquad$  $\dfrac{81}{9} =$  $\qquad$  $\dfrac{43}{13} =$  $\qquad$  $\dfrac{31}{5} =$  $\qquad$  $\dfrac{80}{12} =$

# WRITING IMPROPER FRACTIONS

Mixed and whole numbers can be written as improper fractions.

Write $5\frac{2}{5}$ as an improper fraction.

**Think:** $5\frac{2}{5} = 5 + \frac{2}{5}$

Make 5 into an improper fraction with a denominator of 5.

$5 \times \frac{5}{5} = \frac{5 \times 5}{5} = \frac{25}{5}$

Add $\frac{25}{5} + \frac{2}{5}$.

$\frac{25}{5} + \frac{2}{5} = \frac{25 + 2}{5} = \frac{27}{5}$

$5\frac{2}{5} = \frac{\mathbf{27}}{\mathbf{5}}$

**Write each mixed number as a simplified improper fraction.**

A. $8\frac{2}{3} = $      $5\frac{2}{5} = $      $2\frac{9}{18} = $      $4\frac{3}{8} = $

B. $6\frac{3}{4} = $      $3\frac{3}{37} = $      $10\frac{2}{3} = $      $12\frac{3}{4} = $

C. $10\frac{2}{5} = $      $11\frac{1}{11} = $      $1\frac{7}{16} = $      $8\frac{8}{12} = $

D. $6\frac{10}{12} = $      $3\frac{10}{16} = $      $5\frac{1}{16} = $      $12\frac{7}{12} = $

**Write each whole number as an improper fraction.**

E. $1 = \frac{}{5}$      $1 = \frac{}{12}$      $4 = \frac{}{2}$      $6 = \frac{}{4}$

F. $8 = \frac{}{3}$      $10 = \frac{}{3}$      $12 = \frac{}{5}$      $16 = \frac{}{2}$

G. $18 = \frac{}{3}$      $11 = \frac{}{5}$      $13 = \frac{}{2}$      $15 = \frac{}{5}$

# ADDING AND SUBTRACTING FRACTIONS WITH LIKE DENOMINATORS

$\dfrac{1}{8} + \dfrac{3}{8}$ and $\dfrac{7}{8} - \dfrac{3}{8}$

| Add or subtract the numerators to find the numerator of the answer. | Write the denominator of the fractions as the denominator of the answer. | Simplify if possible. |
| --- | --- | --- |
| $\dfrac{1}{8} + \dfrac{3}{8} = \dfrac{4}{\quad}$ | $\dfrac{1}{8} + \dfrac{3}{8} = \dfrac{4}{8}$ | $\dfrac{1}{8} + \dfrac{3}{8} = \dfrac{4}{8} = \dfrac{1}{2}$ |
| $\dfrac{7}{8} - \dfrac{3}{8} = \dfrac{4}{\quad}$ | $\dfrac{7}{8} - \dfrac{3}{8} = \dfrac{4}{8}$ | $\dfrac{7}{8} - \dfrac{3}{8} = \dfrac{4}{8} = \dfrac{1}{2}$ |

**Solve each problem. Simplify if possible.**

A. $\quad \dfrac{5}{7} - \dfrac{4}{7} =$ $\qquad\qquad \dfrac{3}{10} + \dfrac{7}{10} =$ $\qquad\qquad \dfrac{7}{12} - \dfrac{1}{12} =$

B. $\quad \dfrac{5}{6} + \dfrac{5}{6} =$ $\qquad\qquad \dfrac{2}{15} + \dfrac{8}{15} =$ $\qquad\qquad \dfrac{2}{5} + \dfrac{4}{5} =$

C. $\quad \dfrac{15}{20} - \dfrac{8}{20} =$ $\qquad\qquad \dfrac{10}{11} - \dfrac{4}{11} =$ $\qquad\qquad \dfrac{9}{10} - \dfrac{4}{10} =$

D. $\quad \dfrac{4}{9} + \dfrac{8}{9} =$ $\qquad\qquad \dfrac{3}{5} + \dfrac{4}{5} =$ $\qquad\qquad \dfrac{5}{6} + \dfrac{1}{6} =$

E. $\quad \dfrac{9}{10} - \dfrac{3}{10} =$ $\qquad\qquad \dfrac{4}{7} + \dfrac{6}{7} =$ $\qquad\qquad \dfrac{3}{8} - \dfrac{1}{8} =$

F. $\quad \dfrac{7}{8} - \dfrac{4}{8} =$ $\qquad\qquad \dfrac{8}{12} - \dfrac{3}{12} =$ $\qquad\qquad \dfrac{4}{9} - \dfrac{2}{9} =$

# ADDING AND SUBTRACTING MIXED NUMBERS WITH LIKE DENOMINATORS

$2\frac{7}{9} + 4\frac{8}{9}$ and $2\frac{5}{6} - 1\frac{1}{6}$

Add or subtract the numerators. The denominator of the answer is the same as the denominator of the fractions.

Add or subtract the whole numbers.

Simplify if possible.

$\frac{15}{9} = 1\frac{6}{9}$

$1\frac{6}{9} + 6 = 7\frac{6}{9} = \mathbf{7\frac{2}{3}}$

$\frac{4}{6} = \frac{2}{3}$

$1 + \frac{2}{3} = 1\mathbf{\frac{2}{3}}$

$\begin{array}{r} 2\frac{7}{9} \\ + \ 4\frac{8}{9} \\ \hline \frac{15}{9} \end{array}$
$\begin{array}{r} 2\frac{5}{6} \\ - \ 1\frac{1}{6} \\ \hline \frac{4}{6} \end{array}$
$\begin{array}{r} 2\frac{7}{9} \\ + \ 4\frac{8}{9} \\ \hline 6\frac{15}{9} \end{array}$
$\begin{array}{r} 2\frac{5}{6} \\ - \ 1\frac{1}{6} \\ \hline 1\frac{4}{6} \end{array}$

**Solve each problem. Simplify if possible.**

A.
$\begin{array}{r} 3\frac{1}{3} \\ + \ 1\frac{2}{3} \\ \hline \end{array}$
$\begin{array}{r} 6\frac{7}{10} \\ - \ 2\frac{3}{10} \\ \hline \end{array}$
$\begin{array}{r} 4\frac{5}{6} \\ - \ \ \frac{1}{6} \\ \hline \end{array}$
$\begin{array}{r} 4\frac{7}{8} \\ + \ 1\frac{1}{8} \\ \hline \end{array}$
$\begin{array}{r} 2\frac{4}{9} \\ - \ 1\frac{1}{9} \\ \hline \end{array}$

B.
$\begin{array}{r} 4\frac{1}{2} \\ + \ 4\frac{1}{2} \\ \hline \end{array}$
$\begin{array}{r} 5\frac{2}{3} \\ - \ 4 \\ \hline \end{array}$
$\begin{array}{r} 3\frac{1}{2} \\ - \ 1\frac{1}{2} \\ \hline \end{array}$
$\begin{array}{r} 3\frac{7}{12} \\ - \ 2\frac{1}{12} \\ \hline \end{array}$
$\begin{array}{r} 6\frac{4}{5} \\ + \ 3\frac{3}{5} \\ \hline \end{array}$

C.
$\begin{array}{r} 7\frac{3}{5} \\ - \ 5 \\ \hline \end{array}$
$\begin{array}{r} 6\frac{3}{4} \\ + \ \ \frac{3}{4} \\ \hline \end{array}$
$\begin{array}{r} 5\frac{11}{14} \\ - \ 2\frac{3}{14} \\ \hline \end{array}$
$\begin{array}{r} 8\frac{3}{15} \\ + \ 7\frac{1}{15} \\ \hline \end{array}$
$\begin{array}{r} 6\frac{9}{10} \\ + \ 2\frac{7}{10} \\ \hline \end{array}$

 **MATH SUCCESS** RB-904108

# RENAMING AND SUBTRACTING MIXED NUMBERS WITH LIKE DENOMINATORS

When the numerator of the larger mixed number is smaller than the numerator of the smaller mixed number, one way to solve the problem is to rename the mixed number before you subtract.

$7\frac{1}{9} - 2\frac{4}{9}$

Since $\frac{1}{9} < \frac{4}{9}$, rename $7\frac{1}{9}$ as a whole number and an improper fraction.

$7\frac{1}{9} = 6 + \frac{9}{9} + \frac{1}{9} = 6\frac{10}{9}$

Subtract. Simplify if possible.

$$
\begin{array}{r}
6\frac{10}{9} \\
-\ 2\frac{4}{9} \\
\hline
4\frac{6}{9} = \mathbf{4\frac{2}{3}}
\end{array}
$$

**Solve each problem. Simplify if possible.**

A.

$$
\begin{array}{r}
7\frac{3}{9} \\
-\ 2\frac{4}{9} \\
\hline
\end{array}
\qquad
\begin{array}{r}
2\frac{5}{8} \\
-\ \frac{7}{8} \\
\hline
\end{array}
\qquad
\begin{array}{r}
5\frac{1}{6} \\
-\ 2\frac{5}{6} \\
\hline
\end{array}
\qquad
\begin{array}{r}
7\frac{1}{4} \\
-\ 3\frac{3}{4} \\
\hline
\end{array}
\qquad
\begin{array}{r}
14\frac{3}{5} \\
-\ 8\frac{4}{5} \\
\hline
\end{array}
$$

B.

$$
\begin{array}{r}
4\frac{3}{7} \\
-\ 1\frac{5}{7} \\
\hline
\end{array}
\qquad
\begin{array}{r}
6\frac{4}{15} \\
-\ 4\frac{7}{15} \\
\hline
\end{array}
\qquad
\begin{array}{r}
8\frac{2}{5} \\
-\ 3\frac{4}{5} \\
\hline
\end{array}
\qquad
\begin{array}{r}
7\frac{3}{8} \\
-\ 1\frac{5}{8} \\
\hline
\end{array}
\qquad
\begin{array}{r}
16\frac{6}{8} \\
-\ 9\frac{7}{8} \\
\hline
\end{array}
$$

C.

$$
\begin{array}{r}
9 \\
-\ 3\frac{2}{8} \\
\hline
\end{array}
\qquad
\begin{array}{r}
6 \\
-\ 1\frac{1}{2} \\
\hline
\end{array}
\qquad
\begin{array}{r}
5 \\
-\ 2\frac{3}{4} \\
\hline
\end{array}
\qquad
\begin{array}{r}
30\frac{5}{9} \\
-\ 18\frac{7}{9} \\
\hline
\end{array}
\qquad
\begin{array}{r}
18\frac{3}{9} \\
-\ 4\frac{7}{9} \\
\hline
\end{array}
$$

## RENAMING AND SUBTRACTING MIXED NUMBERS WITH LIKE DENOMINATORS

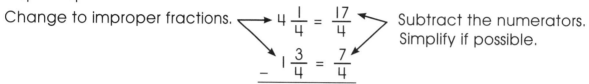

Another way to subtract mixed numbers is to change them to improper fractions.

$4\frac{1}{4} - 1\frac{3}{4}$

Change to improper fractions. $4\frac{1}{4} = \frac{17}{4}$   Subtract the numerators. Simplify if possible.

$1\frac{3}{4} = \frac{7}{4}$

$\frac{10}{4} = 2\frac{2}{4} = \mathbf{2\frac{1}{2}}$

**Solve each problem. Simplify if possible.**

A.
$$8\frac{1}{5}$$
$$-\ 3\frac{4}{5}$$

$$6\frac{1}{8}$$
$$-\ 1\frac{2}{8}$$

$$9\frac{1}{9}$$
$$-\ 3\frac{6}{9}$$

B.
$$5\frac{2}{5}$$
$$-\ 2\frac{3}{5}$$

$$4\frac{2}{8}$$
$$-\ 3\frac{6}{8}$$

$$7\frac{2}{4}$$
$$-\ 4\frac{3}{4}$$

C.
$$10\frac{3}{8}$$
$$-\ 6\frac{5}{8}$$

$$6\frac{3}{6}$$
$$-\ 2\frac{5}{6}$$

$$14\frac{2}{6}$$
$$-\ 4\frac{4}{6}$$

D.
$$14\frac{3}{5}$$
$$-\ 8\frac{4}{5}$$

$$16\frac{6}{8}$$
$$-\ 9\frac{7}{8}$$

$$14\frac{2}{5}$$
$$-\ 4\frac{4}{5}$$

**MATH SUCCESS** RB-904108

# ADDING AND SUBTRACTING FRACTIONS WITH UNLIKE DENOMINATORS

Rewrite the fractions using the least common denominator. Then, add or subtract the numerators. Write the answer as a mixed number or a fraction in simplest form.

$$\frac{5}{6}$$     $$\frac{5}{6} = \frac{10}{12}$$     $$\frac{4}{5}$$     $$\frac{4}{5} = \frac{24}{30}$$

$$+\frac{3}{4}$$     $$+\frac{3}{4} = \frac{9}{12}$$     $$-\frac{2}{6}$$     $$-\frac{2}{6} = \frac{10}{30}$$

$$\frac{19}{12} = 1\frac{7}{12}$$     $$\frac{14}{30} = \frac{7}{15}$$

**Solve each problem. Simplify if possible.**

A.    $$\frac{2}{3}$$     $$\frac{5}{6}$$     $$\frac{2}{5}$$     $$\frac{3}{8}$$     $$\frac{2}{3}$$

    $$+\frac{1}{4}$$     $$-\frac{4}{9}$$     $$+\frac{7}{10}$$     $$-\frac{1}{4}$$     $$-\frac{4}{9}$$

B.    $$\frac{3}{8}$$     $$\frac{1}{2}$$     $$\frac{2}{3}$$     $$\frac{3}{10}$$     $$\frac{5}{6}$$

    $$+\frac{5}{6}$$     $$+\frac{7}{8}$$     $$-\frac{3}{5}$$     $$+\frac{3}{4}$$     $$-\frac{1}{7}$$

C.    $$\frac{1}{2}$$     $$\frac{1}{2}$$     $$\frac{3}{10}$$     $$\frac{2}{3}$$     $$\frac{1}{8}$$

    $$-\frac{3}{10}$$     $$+\frac{4}{5}$$     $$-\frac{1}{6}$$     $$+\frac{5}{9}$$     $$+\frac{4}{5}$$

D.    $$\frac{1}{6}$$     $$\frac{2}{15}$$     $$\frac{5}{12}$$     $$\frac{4}{7}$$     $$\frac{6}{7}$$

    $$-\frac{1}{12}$$     $$+\frac{1}{6}$$     $$-\frac{1}{4}$$     $$+\frac{6}{9}$$     $$-\frac{2}{5}$$

# ADDING MIXED NUMBERS WITH UNLIKE DENOMINATORS

$4\frac{5}{6} + 1\frac{3}{9}$

| Rewrite the fractions using the LCD. | Add the numerators. | Add the whole numbers. | Simplify if possible. |
|---|---|---|---|
| $4\frac{5}{6} = 4\frac{15}{18}$ <br> $+\ 1\frac{3}{9} = 1\frac{6}{18}$ | $4\frac{5}{6} = 4\frac{\mathbf{15}}{18}$ <br> $+\ 1\frac{3}{9} = 1\frac{\mathbf{6}}{18}$ <br> $\frac{\mathbf{21}}{18}$ | $4\frac{5}{6} = \mathbf{4}\frac{15}{18}$ <br> $+\ 1\frac{3}{9} = \mathbf{1}\frac{6}{18}$ <br> $\mathbf{5}\frac{21}{18}$ | $4\frac{5}{6} = 4\frac{15}{18}$ <br> $+\ 1\frac{3}{9} = 1\frac{6}{18}$ <br> $5\frac{21}{18} = \mathbf{6}\frac{\mathbf{1}}{\mathbf{6}}$ |

## Solve each problem. Simplify if possible.

A.

$4\frac{2}{3}$    $7\frac{5}{4}$    $6\frac{7}{8}$    $9\frac{3}{4}$    $2\frac{3}{4}$

$+\ 3\frac{1}{2}$    $+\ 5\frac{1}{6}$    $+\ 2\frac{3}{4}$    $+\ 7\frac{2}{5}$    $+\ 1\frac{1}{6}$

B.

$12\frac{7}{8}$    $36\frac{1}{2}$    $15\frac{5}{9}$    $6\frac{10}{18}$    $8\frac{2}{3}$

$+\ 6\frac{1}{3}$    $+\ 25\frac{3}{10}$    $+\ 9\frac{1}{3}$    $+\ 2\frac{2}{9}$    $+\ 5\frac{1}{4}$

C.

$8\frac{3}{8}$    $9\frac{7}{8}$    $4\frac{1}{2}$    $15\frac{3}{4}$    $8\frac{1}{3}$

$+\ 5\frac{1}{6}$    $+\ 4\frac{5}{6}$    $+\ 2\frac{1}{3}$    $+\ 12\frac{5}{8}$    $+\ 6\frac{1}{6}$

# RENAMING AND SUBTRACTING MIXED NUMBERS WITH UNLIKE DENOMINATORS

$8 \dfrac{4}{6} - 3 \dfrac{4}{9}$

| Rewrite the fractions using the least common denominator. | Subtract the numerators. | Subtract the whole numbers. | Simplify if possible. |
|---|---|---|---|
| $8 \dfrac{4}{6} = 8 \dfrac{12}{18}$ <br> $- \ 3 \dfrac{4}{9} = 3 \dfrac{8}{18}$ | $8 \dfrac{4}{6} = 8 \dfrac{\mathbf{12}}{18}$ <br> $- \ 3 \dfrac{4}{9} = 3 \dfrac{\mathbf{8}}{18}$ <br> $\dfrac{4}{18}$ | $8 \dfrac{4}{6} = \mathbf{8} \dfrac{12}{18}$ <br> $- \ 3 \dfrac{3}{9} = \mathbf{3} \dfrac{8}{18}$ <br> $\mathbf{5} \dfrac{4}{18}$ | $8 \dfrac{4}{6} = 8 \dfrac{12}{18}$ <br> $- \ 3 \dfrac{3}{9} = 3 \dfrac{8}{18}$ <br> $5 \dfrac{4}{18} = \mathbf{5} \dfrac{\mathbf{2}}{\mathbf{9}}$ |

**Solve each problem. Simplify if possible.**

A.
$6 \dfrac{1}{4}$ $\qquad$ $7 \dfrac{1}{7}$ $\qquad$ $8 \dfrac{1}{3}$ $\qquad$ $8 \dfrac{1}{4}$
$- \ 4 \dfrac{7}{16}$ $\qquad$ $- \ 3 \dfrac{6}{14}$ $\qquad$ $- \ 2 \dfrac{9}{15}$ $\qquad$ $- \ 4 \dfrac{6}{8}$

B.
$9 \dfrac{1}{18}$ $\qquad$ $3 \dfrac{1}{10}$ $\qquad$ $5 \dfrac{1}{16}$ $\qquad$ $9 \dfrac{2}{5}$
$- \ 5 \dfrac{3}{6}$ $\qquad$ $- \ 1 \dfrac{4}{5}$ $\qquad$ $- \ 4 \dfrac{6}{8}$ $\qquad$ $- \ 5 \dfrac{3}{4}$

C.
$25 \dfrac{9}{18}$ $\qquad$ $14 \dfrac{3}{8}$ $\qquad$ $18 \dfrac{2}{6}$ $\qquad$ $12 \dfrac{1}{6}$
$- \ 17 \dfrac{2}{6}$ $\qquad$ $- \ 1 \dfrac{8}{16}$ $\qquad$ $- \ 5 \dfrac{9}{15}$ $\qquad$ $- \ 8 \dfrac{4}{7}$

# ADDING AND SUBTRACTING FRACTIONS PROBLEM SOLVING

**Use the recipe to solve each problem. Simplify if possible.**

> ## TRAIL MIX
>
> $1\frac{1}{4}$ cups sunflower seeds
>
> $1\frac{1}{2}$ cups peanuts
>
> $\frac{3}{4}$ cup candy-coated chocolate pieces
>
> $\frac{5}{8}$ cup raisins
>
> Mix all ingredients. (Makes 1 batch.)

A. Mrs. Johnson plans to make a batch of trail mix, and she would like to add extra raisins. If she doubles the amount of raisins in the recipe, how many cups of raisins will she need?

_____

B. After measuring the amount of peanuts needed to make a batch of trail mix, Mrs. Johnson had $2\frac{1}{2}$ cups of peanuts left over. How many cups of peanuts did she begin with?

_____

C. Mrs. Johnson increased the amount of candy-coated chocolate pieces in the recipe to $1\frac{1}{8}$ cups. How many more cups of chocolate pieces did she use than the recipe required?

_____

D. If none of the measurements are altered, how many cups of trail mix does one batch make?

_____

**MATH SUCCESS** RB-904108 © Rainbow Bridge Publishing

# ADDING AND SUBTRACTING FRACTIONS PROBLEM SOLVING

**Solve each problem. Simplify if possible.**

A. In a baseball league, the Tigers are $1\frac{1}{2}$ games behind the Pirates, and the Pirates are 4 games ahead of the Jaguars. How many games separate the Tigers and the Jaguars?

_____

B. Softball bats are $2\frac{1}{2}$ inches in diameter. If a softball is $3\frac{1}{8}$ in diameter, how much wider is the softball than the bat?

_____

C. Suppose $\frac{5}{8}$ of major league baseball fans watch the games on television, and $\frac{1}{3}$ of the fans listen to them on the radio. Fractionally, how many more baseball fans watch the games on television than listen to them on the radio?

_____

D. Bob spent $\frac{3}{8}$ of his birthday money at a baseball game and $\frac{5}{12}$ on a new bat and glove. What fraction of his birthday money did Bob spend?

_____

# ADDING AND SUBTRACTING FRACTIONS ASSESSMENT

**Write an improper fraction for each mixed number.**

A.  $2\frac{1}{3}$ =          $4\frac{3}{8}$ =          $6\frac{3}{5}$ =          $11\frac{5}{6}$ =

**Write a mixed number for each improper fraction. Simplify if possible.**

B.  $\dfrac{23}{7}$ =          $\dfrac{52}{8}$ =          $\dfrac{15}{2}$ =          $\dfrac{85}{16}$ =

**Solve each problem. Simplify if possible.**

C.

$$\begin{array}{r} \frac{1}{5} \\ + \ \frac{3}{5} \\ \hline \end{array} \qquad \begin{array}{r} \frac{3}{8} \\ + \ \frac{7}{8} \\ \hline \end{array} \qquad \begin{array}{r} \frac{2}{3} \\ + \ \frac{2}{5} \\ \hline \end{array} \qquad \begin{array}{r} \frac{7}{18} \\ + \ \frac{12}{36} \\ \hline \end{array}$$

D.

$$\begin{array}{r} \frac{5}{6} \\ - \ \frac{1}{6} \\ \hline \end{array} \qquad \begin{array}{r} \frac{5}{6} \\ - \ \frac{1}{4} \\ \hline \end{array} \qquad \begin{array}{r} \frac{11}{12} \\ - \ \frac{4}{5} \\ \hline \end{array} \qquad \begin{array}{r} \frac{6}{10} \\ - \ \frac{4}{15} \\ \hline \end{array}$$

E.

$$\begin{array}{r} 9\frac{2}{3} \\ + \ 1\frac{1}{3} \\ \hline \end{array} \qquad \begin{array}{r} 2\frac{1}{2} \\ + \ 2\frac{3}{5} \\ \hline \end{array} \qquad \begin{array}{r} 8\frac{1}{4} \\ - \ 3\frac{5}{6} \\ \hline \end{array} \qquad \begin{array}{r} 9\frac{5}{6} \\ - \ 4\frac{5}{7} \\ \hline \end{array}$$

**Solve each problem. Write answers in simplest form.**

F.  Robert recorded a $2\frac{1}{2}$ hour movie and a $1\frac{3}{4}$ hour movie on one DVD. How many hours of movies are on the DVD? _____

G.  The rainfall in Jane's town totaled $6\frac{1}{4}$ inches in April and $4\frac{1}{16}$ inches in May. How much more rain fell in April than in May? _____

**MATH SUCCESS** RB-904108                    © Rainbow Bridge Publishing

**Write an improper fraction for each mixed number.**

A.   $1\dfrac{2}{5} =$        $5\dfrac{3}{4} =$        $3\dfrac{5}{6} =$        $12\dfrac{7}{8} =$

**Write a mixed number for each improper fraction. Simplify if possible.**

B.   $\dfrac{28}{5} =$        $\dfrac{38}{6} =$        $\dfrac{30}{9} =$        $\dfrac{48}{10} =$

**Solve each problem. Simplify if possible.**

C.
$$\dfrac{3}{7} + \dfrac{2}{7}\qquad \dfrac{5}{6} + \dfrac{3}{6}\qquad \dfrac{3}{4} + \dfrac{2}{5}\qquad \dfrac{21}{25} + \dfrac{2}{10}$$

D.
$$\dfrac{6}{7} - \dfrac{3}{7}\qquad \dfrac{3}{4} - \dfrac{1}{3}\qquad \dfrac{9}{12} - \dfrac{3}{5}\qquad \dfrac{3}{5} - \dfrac{2}{9}$$

E.
$$6\dfrac{1}{4} + 2\dfrac{3}{4}\qquad 3\dfrac{3}{5} + 5\dfrac{7}{10}\qquad 6\dfrac{1}{9} - 1\dfrac{5}{8}\qquad 18\dfrac{4}{9} - 9\dfrac{6}{9}$$

**Solve each problem. Simplify if possible.**

F.   Rita's video collection is $\dfrac{1}{3}$ comedy videos and $\dfrac{1}{5}$ adventure videos. What part of Rita's video collection is neither comedy nor adventure?

_____

G.   A total of 4 inches of rain was predicted for the month of June, but only $2\dfrac{3}{8}$ inches actually fell. What is the difference between the predicted rainfall and the actual rainfall? _____

# MULTIPLYING FRACTIONS

$\dfrac{3}{4}$ x $\dfrac{2}{8}$

Multiply the numerators. Then, multiply the denominators.

Simplify if possible.

$\dfrac{3}{4}$ x $\dfrac{2}{8}$ = $\dfrac{\mathbf{3 \times 2}}{\mathbf{4 \times 8}}$ = $\dfrac{6}{32}$

$\dfrac{6}{32}$ = $\dfrac{\mathbf{3}}{\mathbf{16}}$

**Solve each problem. Simplify if possible.**

A.  $\dfrac{1}{8}$ x $\dfrac{1}{5}$ =     $\dfrac{1}{4}$ x $\dfrac{1}{7}$ =     $\dfrac{1}{12}$ x $\dfrac{1}{8}$ =

B.  $\dfrac{3}{7}$ x $\dfrac{4}{5}$ =     $\dfrac{4}{5}$ x $\dfrac{6}{8}$ =     $\dfrac{2}{3}$ x $\dfrac{4}{7}$ =

C.  $\dfrac{5}{6}$ x $\dfrac{4}{5}$ =     $\dfrac{2}{3}$ x $\dfrac{7}{8}$ =     $\dfrac{7}{9}$ x $\dfrac{8}{9}$ =

D.  $\dfrac{1}{2}$ x $\dfrac{2}{12}$ =     $\dfrac{2}{3}$ x $\dfrac{4}{12}$ =     $\dfrac{6}{8}$ x $\dfrac{4}{16}$ =

E.  $\dfrac{7}{10}$ x $\dfrac{3}{5}$ =     $\dfrac{2}{7}$ x $\dfrac{10}{14}$ =     $\dfrac{4}{6}$ x $\dfrac{12}{18}$ =

F.  $\dfrac{12}{16}$ x $\dfrac{3}{7}$ =     $\dfrac{6}{12}$ x $\dfrac{5}{6}$ =     $\dfrac{2}{4}$ x $\dfrac{10}{12}$ =

# MULTIPLYING FRACTIONS BY WHOLE NUMBERS

$\frac{2}{3} \times 4$

Write the whole number as a fraction. Any whole number can be converted to a fraction by writing 1 as the denominator.

Multiply the numerators. Then, multiply the denominators.

Change the improper fraction to a simplified mixed number.

$\frac{2}{3} \times 4 = \frac{2}{3} \times \frac{4}{1}$

$\frac{2}{3} \times \frac{4}{1} = \frac{2 \times 4}{3 \times 1} = \frac{8}{3}$

$\frac{8}{3} = 2\frac{2}{3}$

## Solve each problem. Simplify if possible.

A.    $\frac{1}{15} \times 5 =$        $\frac{5}{14} \times 7 =$        $\frac{1}{16} \times 8 =$

B.    $\frac{6}{15} \times 4 =$        $\frac{5}{12} \times 6 =$        $\frac{3}{16} \times 8 =$

C.    $\frac{9}{12} \times 3 =$        $\frac{4}{18} \times 6 =$        $\frac{5}{15} \times 10 =$

D.    $2 \times \frac{9}{10} =$        $6 \times \frac{3}{18} =$        $4 \times \frac{6}{16} =$

E.    $3 \times \frac{4}{15} =$        $5 \times \frac{10}{12} =$        $5 \times \frac{3}{6} =$

F.    $3 \times \frac{5}{11} =$        $2 \times \frac{7}{12} =$        $2 \times \frac{12}{13} =$

## MULTIPLYING FRACTIONS BY MIXED NUMBERS

$\frac{3}{4} \times 4\frac{4}{5}$

| Write the mixed number as an improper fraction. | Multiply the numerators. Then, multiply the denominators. | Change the improper fraction to a simplified mixed number. |
|---|---|---|
| $\frac{3}{4} \times 4\frac{4}{5} = \frac{3}{4} \times \frac{\mathbf{24}}{\mathbf{5}}$ | $\frac{3}{4} \times \frac{24}{5} = \frac{\mathbf{3 \times 24}}{\mathbf{4 \times 5}} = \frac{72}{20}$ | $\frac{72}{20} = 3\frac{12}{20} = \mathbf{3\frac{3}{5}}$ |

**Solve each problem. Simplify if possible.**

A. $\frac{1}{3} \times 3\frac{1}{4} =$  $\qquad$ $\frac{1}{2} \times 2\frac{1}{5} =$  $\qquad$ $\frac{2}{4} \times 2\frac{1}{6} =$

B. $\frac{3}{6} \times 4\frac{3}{4} =$  $\qquad$ $\frac{4}{8} \times 5\frac{2}{3} =$  $\qquad$ $6\frac{1}{3} \times \frac{1}{8} =$

C. $2\frac{3}{4} \times \frac{3}{5} =$  $\qquad$ $4\frac{2}{5} \times \frac{3}{4} =$  $\qquad$ $1\frac{2}{7} \times \frac{2}{4} =$

D. $\frac{1}{10} \times 5\frac{1}{4} =$  $\qquad$ $\frac{1}{5} \times 4\frac{1}{2} =$  $\qquad$ $\frac{2}{15} \times 10\frac{2}{4} =$

E. $7\frac{1}{2} \times \frac{1}{12} =$  $\qquad$ $3\frac{1}{4} \times \frac{1}{13} =$  $\qquad$ $2\frac{3}{4} \times \frac{2}{11} =$

F. $\frac{3}{11} \times 2\frac{2}{8} =$  $\qquad$ $\frac{4}{10} \times 3\frac{2}{6} =$  $\qquad$ $\frac{4}{15} \times 1\frac{5}{8} =$

**MATH SUCCESS** RB-904108

# MULTIPLYING MIXED NUMBERS

$1\frac{2}{3} \times 4\frac{2}{5}$

Write each mixed number as an improper fraction.

$1\frac{2}{3} = \frac{5}{3}$

$4\frac{2}{5} = \frac{22}{5}$

Multiply the numerators. Then, multiply the denominators.

$\frac{5}{3} \times \frac{22}{5} = \frac{5 \times 22}{3 \times 5} = \frac{110}{15}$

Change the improper fraction to a simplified mixed number.

$\frac{110}{15} = 7\frac{5}{15} = 7\frac{1}{3}$

**Solve each problem. Simplify if possible.**

A. $3\frac{1}{3} \times 4\frac{1}{4} =$ $\qquad$ $2\frac{1}{5} \times 1\frac{1}{6} =$ $\qquad$ $2\frac{1}{4} \times 2\frac{1}{2} =$

B. $1\frac{1}{6} \times 2\frac{1}{7} =$ $\qquad$ $4\frac{1}{8} \times 1\frac{1}{8} =$ $\qquad$ $3\frac{1}{2} \times 3\frac{3}{4} =$

C. $1\frac{1}{4} \times 3\frac{2}{5} =$ $\qquad$ $2\frac{1}{3} \times 1\frac{6}{8} =$ $\qquad$ $2\frac{4}{5} \times 3\frac{1}{6} =$

D. $3\frac{2}{8} \times 1\frac{1}{2} =$ $\qquad$ $2\frac{3}{7} \times 2\frac{1}{4} =$ $\qquad$ $1\frac{2}{7} \times 2\frac{2}{5} =$

E. $2\frac{3}{5} \times 3\frac{2}{4} =$ $\qquad$ $1\frac{2}{9} \times 1\frac{3}{5} =$ $\qquad$ $1\frac{1}{16} \times 2\frac{1}{4} =$

F. $1\frac{3}{7} \times 2\frac{2}{5} =$ $\qquad$ $1\frac{6}{8} \times 2\frac{2}{5} =$ $\qquad$ $1\frac{1}{12} \times 1\frac{1}{3} =$

# MULTIPLYING WHOLE NUMBERS BY MIXED NUMBERS

$5 \times 6\frac{4}{7}$

Write both numbers as improper fractions.

$5 = \frac{5}{1}$

$6\frac{4}{7} = \frac{46}{7}$

Multiply the numerators. Then, multiply the denominators.

$\frac{5}{1} \times \frac{46}{7} = \frac{5 \times 46}{1 \times 7} = \frac{230}{7}$

Change the improper fraction to a simplified mixed number or whole number.

$\frac{230}{7} = 32\frac{6}{7}$

**Solve each problem. Simplify if possible.**

A. $6 \times 2\frac{1}{3} =$          $7 \times 2\frac{1}{5} =$          $3 \times 2\frac{1}{5} =$

B. $2 \times 1\frac{3}{8} =$          $5 \times 4\frac{2}{4} =$          $6 \times 2\frac{4}{5} =$

C. $2\frac{1}{3} \times 3 =$          $1\frac{1}{8} \times 5 =$          $1\frac{1}{4} \times 6 =$

D. $3\frac{3}{7} \times 2 =$          $2\frac{4}{5} \times 3 =$          $2\frac{3}{4} \times 4 =$

E. $1\frac{3}{9} \times 5 =$          $1\frac{5}{8} \times 2 =$          $6 \times 2\frac{2}{5} =$

F. $8 \times 3\frac{1}{5} =$          $1\frac{2}{4} \times 3 =$          $2\frac{2}{3} \times 3 =$

# FINDING FRACTIONS OF NUMBERS

In mathematics, the word **of** is the same as **times**.

"What is $\frac{2}{3}$ of 51?" means "What is $\frac{2}{3}$ **x** 51?"

Remember, **of** means "multiply."

Turn the whole number into a fraction by writing a 1 as the denominator.

$\frac{2}{3} \times 51 = \frac{2}{3} \times \frac{51}{1}$

Multiply the numerators. Multiply the denominators.

$\frac{2}{3} \times \frac{51}{1} = \frac{2 \times 51}{3 \times 1} = \frac{102}{3}$

Remember, the fraction bar is also a division bar.

$\frac{102}{3} = 3\overline{)102} = 34$

**So, $\frac{2}{3}$ of 51 is 34.**

**Solve each problem. Simplify if possible.**

A.  $\frac{2}{5}$ of 10        $\frac{5}{6}$ of 24        $\frac{4}{5}$ of 60        $\frac{3}{4}$ of 44

B.  $\frac{7}{10}$ of 80        $\frac{6}{25}$ of 125        $\frac{5}{8}$ of 96        $\frac{7}{12}$ of 144

C.  $\frac{1}{2}$ of 15        $\frac{2}{3}$ of 32        $\frac{3}{4}$ of 78        $\frac{1}{8}$ of 74

D.  $\frac{5}{8}$ of 20        $\frac{1}{3}$ of 22        $\frac{1}{6}$ of 50        $\frac{9}{10}$ of 35

**Solve each problem. Simplify if possible.**

E.  Four-sevenths of the students in Mrs. Mason's sixth-grade class are girls. If there are 28 students in Mrs. Mason's class, how many of them are girls?

F.  Three-fifths of the cookies on the tray are chocolate chip. If there are 120 cookies on the tray, how many cookies are chocolate chip?

# MULTIPLYING FRACTIONS PROBLEM SOLVING

**Use the ingredients list from the recipe to solve each problem. Simplify if possible.**

---

## CHILLAQUILLAS
### (serves 6)

I dozen tortillas

$\frac{2}{3}$ cup chopped green onions

$2\frac{1}{2}$ cups grated Monterey Jack cheese

$2\frac{1}{4}$ teaspoons chili powder

$1\frac{1}{3}$ cups tomato sauce

$\frac{1}{2}$ teaspoon crushed oregano

$1\frac{1}{4}$ cups low-fat cottage cheese

$\frac{1}{4}$ cup oil

---

A. Carl will need enough chillaquillas to serve 8 people. What mixed number should the recipe be multiplied by to make enough for 8 people?

B. How much tomato sauce is required if the recipe is doubled?

C. How many cups of chopped green onions will be needed if the recipe is tripled?

D. Carl's recipe instructs him to bake at 205°C (degrees Celsius). He can convert this temperature to degrees Fahrenheit (°F) using this formula: °F = $\frac{9}{5}$ x °C + 32. What cooking temperature should he use in degrees Fahrenheit?

# MULTIPLYING FRACTIONS PROBLEM SOLVING

Drawing a model can help solve problems with fractions.

**Example:** In one year, a pond dries up to $\frac{1}{3}$ of its size. In the next year, it dries up to $\frac{1}{3}$ of that size. What fraction of the original pond is left?

Year 1

Year 2

Year 3

After the first year, the pond is $\frac{1}{3}$ of one whole, or $\frac{1}{3}$ x 1 = $\frac{1}{3}$ . After the second year, the pond is $\frac{1}{3}$ of $\frac{1}{3}$ , or $\frac{1}{3}$ x $\frac{1}{3}$ = $\frac{1}{9}$ .

**Solve each problem by drawing a model. Simplify if possible.**

A.  Suppose every bounce of a ball is $\frac{2}{3}$ of the height of its previous bounce. What fraction of the original height will the height of the third bounce be? _____

Bounce 1

Bounce 2

Bounce 3

B.  Each day, Tina studies for $\frac{1}{2}$ of the number of minutes that she did the previous day. If she studies for 32 minutes on day 1, how many minutes will she study on day 3? _____

C.  An endangered bird species decreases in population size each year. Every year, the number of birds is $\frac{2}{5}$ of what it was the previous year. If there were 900 birds in the year 2001, how many birds were there after the year 2003? _____

**Solve each problem. Simplify if possible.**

A.  $\dfrac{1}{4} \times \dfrac{1}{4} =$    $\dfrac{3}{10} \times \dfrac{1}{12} =$    $\dfrac{4}{7} \times \dfrac{2}{3} =$    $\dfrac{3}{4} \times \dfrac{6}{8} =$

B.  $\dfrac{3}{4} \times \dfrac{4}{5} =$    $\dfrac{3}{7} \times \dfrac{4}{5} =$    $\dfrac{2}{3} \times 9 =$    $\dfrac{4}{6} \times 7 =$

C.  $4 \times \dfrac{10}{16} =$    $\dfrac{10}{15} \times 3 =$    $\dfrac{3}{4} \times 2\dfrac{3}{5} =$    $\dfrac{2}{3} \times 3\dfrac{2}{6} =$

D.  $1\dfrac{3}{9} \times \dfrac{2}{3} =$    $1\dfrac{2}{8} \times \dfrac{2}{4} =$    $2\dfrac{1}{4} \times 3\dfrac{1}{5} =$    $1\dfrac{1}{3} \times 1\dfrac{1}{6} =$

E.  $2\dfrac{3}{5} \times 1\dfrac{2}{3} =$    $3\dfrac{3}{4} \times 2\dfrac{3}{5} =$    $2\dfrac{1}{3} \times 6 =$    $1\dfrac{4}{6} \times 4 =$

**Solve each problem. Simplify if possible.**

F.  Sterling travels $2\dfrac{1}{8}$ miles each day on his paper route. How many miles does he travel in 5 days?

_____

G.  Sterling delivers 35 newspapers, $\dfrac{2}{5}$ of which are delivered on his street. How many newspapers does he deliver on his street?

_____

**Solve each problem. Simplify if possible.**

A.    $\dfrac{1}{6} \times \dfrac{4}{5} =$      $\dfrac{4}{7} \times \dfrac{1}{3} =$      $\dfrac{1}{3} \times \dfrac{5}{7} =$      $\dfrac{5}{6} \times \dfrac{3}{7} =$

B.    $\dfrac{3}{4} \times \dfrac{8}{9} =$      $\dfrac{5}{6} \times \dfrac{3}{5} =$      $\dfrac{12}{13} \times \dfrac{2}{3} =$      $\dfrac{4}{5} \times \dfrac{10}{11} =$

C.    $3 \times \dfrac{3}{16} =$      $\dfrac{10}{12} \times 4 =$      $\dfrac{1}{6} \times 8\dfrac{3}{4} =$      $\dfrac{5}{8} \times 5\dfrac{7}{8} =$

D.    $1\dfrac{1}{3} \times \dfrac{5}{6} =$      $1\dfrac{1}{5} \times \dfrac{1}{4} =$      $\dfrac{2}{5} \times 3\dfrac{1}{3} =$      $2\dfrac{2}{9} \times 1\dfrac{3}{5} =$

E.    $2\dfrac{5}{8} \times 5 =$      $4 \times 2\dfrac{2}{11} =$      $2\dfrac{1}{4} \times 5\dfrac{1}{2} =$      $1\dfrac{3}{11} \times 2\dfrac{12}{13} =$

**Solve each problem. Simplify if possible.**

F.   Madeline needs $2\dfrac{1}{8}$ yards of fabric to make a duffel bag. How much fabric does she need to make 3 duffel bags?

_____

G.   Tanner can make a small gym bag from $1\dfrac{1}{8}$ yards of fabric. How much fabric does Tanner need to make 12 gym bags?

_____

    

# RECIPROCALS

**Reciprocals** are numbers that, when multiplied, have a product of 1. To divide fractions, you must first find the reciprocal of the divisor.

$\frac{7}{4}$

To write the reciprocal of $\frac{7}{4}$, reverse the numerator and the denominator.

$\frac{7}{4} \diagup\!\!\!\!\diagdown \mathbf{\frac{4}{7}}$

To check your answer, multiply the original number by its reciprocal. If the product is 1, the reciprocal is correct.

$\frac{7}{4} \times \frac{4}{7} = \frac{28}{28} = \mathbf{1}$

$4\frac{1}{3}$

To write the reciprocal of $4\frac{1}{3}$, write $4\frac{1}{3}$ as an improper fraction.

$4\frac{1}{3} = \mathbf{\frac{13}{3}}$

Reverse the numerator and the denominator.

$\frac{13}{3} \diagup\!\!\!\!\diagdown \mathbf{\frac{3}{13}}$

To check your answer, multiply the original number by its reciprocal. If the product is 1, the reciprocal is correct.

$4\frac{1}{3} = \frac{13}{3} \times \frac{3}{13} = \frac{39}{39} = \mathbf{1}$

**Write the reciprocal of each number or fraction.**

A.　$\frac{11}{5} \times \boxed{\frac{\ }{\ }} = 1$　　$2\frac{1}{4} \times \boxed{\frac{\ }{\ }} = 1$　　$9 \times \boxed{\frac{\ }{\ }} = 1$　　$\frac{3}{10} \times \boxed{\frac{\ }{\ }} = 1$

B.　$\frac{1}{7} \times \boxed{\frac{\ }{\ }} = 1$　　$4\frac{5}{8} \times \boxed{\frac{\ }{\ }} = 1$　　$\frac{15}{11} \times \boxed{\frac{\ }{\ }} = 1$　　$\frac{1}{6} \times \boxed{\frac{\ }{\ }} = 1$

C.　$\frac{3}{4} \times \boxed{\frac{\ }{\ }} = 1$　　$3 \times \boxed{\frac{\ }{\ }} = 1$　　$\frac{9}{4} \times \boxed{\frac{\ }{\ }} = 1$　　$7\frac{5}{8} \times \boxed{\frac{\ }{\ }} = 1$

D.　$5\frac{2}{3} \times \boxed{\frac{\ }{\ }} = 1$　　$\frac{7}{9} \times \boxed{\frac{\ }{\ }} = 1$　　$27 \times \boxed{\frac{\ }{\ }} = 1$　　$2\frac{1}{5} \times \boxed{\frac{\ }{\ }} = 1$

E.　$\frac{1}{3} \times \boxed{\frac{\ }{\ }} = 1$　　$22 \times \boxed{\frac{\ }{\ }} = 1$　　$\frac{10}{7} \times \boxed{\frac{\ }{\ }} = 1$　　$2\frac{1}{8} \times \boxed{\frac{\ }{\ }} = 1$

# DIVIDING BY FRACTIONS

To divide by a fraction, multiply the dividend by the reciprocal of the divisor.

dividend $\longrightarrow \dfrac{4}{5} \div \dfrac{3}{4} \longleftarrow$ divisor

The reciprocal of $\dfrac{3}{4}$ is $\dfrac{4}{3}$.

$\dfrac{4}{5} \times \mathbf{\dfrac{4}{3}} = \dfrac{4 \times 4}{5 \times 3} = \dfrac{16}{15} = 1\dfrac{1}{15}$

**Solve each problem. Simplify if possible.**

A.    $\dfrac{7}{2} \div \dfrac{1}{2} =$      $\dfrac{4}{3} \div \dfrac{2}{3} =$      $\dfrac{6}{4} \div \dfrac{3}{4} =$      $\dfrac{7}{8} \div \dfrac{3}{5} =$

B.    $\dfrac{9}{2} \div \dfrac{1}{3} =$      $\dfrac{8}{3} \div \dfrac{2}{5} =$      $\dfrac{15}{4} \div \dfrac{3}{7} =$      $\dfrac{2}{3} \div \dfrac{3}{7} =$

C.    $\dfrac{5}{6} \div \dfrac{5}{6} =$      $\dfrac{3}{8} \div \dfrac{3}{4} =$      $\dfrac{3}{4} \div \dfrac{5}{2} =$      $\dfrac{4}{5} \div \dfrac{4}{3} =$

D.    $\dfrac{5}{8} \div \dfrac{1}{8} =$      $\dfrac{4}{7} \div \dfrac{2}{7} =$      $\dfrac{5}{8} \div \dfrac{3}{4} =$      $\dfrac{2}{5} \div \dfrac{4}{6} =$

## DIVIDING FRACTIONS AND WHOLE NUMBERS

Dividing a fraction by a whole number:

$\frac{4}{5} \div 8$

Write the whole number as a fraction with a denominator of 1.

$\frac{4}{5} \div 8 = \frac{4}{5} \div \frac{8}{1}$

Multiply the dividend by the reciprocal of the divisor. Simplify if possible.

$\frac{4}{5} \times \frac{1}{8} = \frac{4 \times 1}{5 \times 8} = \frac{4}{40} = \frac{1}{10}$

Dividing a whole number by a fraction:

$5 \div \frac{3}{4}$

Write the whole number as a fraction with a denominator of 1.

$5 \div \frac{3}{4} = \frac{5}{1} \div \frac{3}{4}$

Multiply the dividend by the reciprocal of the divisor. Simplify if possible.

$\frac{5}{1} \times \frac{4}{3} = \frac{5 \times 4}{1 \times 3} = \frac{20}{3} = 6\frac{2}{3}$

**Solve each problem. Simplify if possible.**

A.　　$6 \div \frac{4}{9} =$　　　　　　$5 \div \frac{1}{7} =$　　　　　　$\frac{4}{7} \div 8 =$

B.　　$4 \div \frac{3}{5} =$　　　　　　$\frac{5}{8} \div 5 =$　　　　　　$\frac{9}{10} \div 4 =$

C.　　$\frac{9}{4} \div 6 =$　　　　　　$4 \div \frac{5}{3} =$　　　　　　$\frac{4}{3} \div 5 =$

D.　　$\frac{10}{9} \div 4 =$　　　　　　$\frac{7}{4} \div 3 =$　　　　　　$8 \div \frac{2}{3} =$

# DIVIDING MIXED NUMBERS AND WHOLE NUMBERS

$3\frac{4}{5} \div 2\frac{3}{4}$

Write each mixed number as an improper fraction. If the dividend or the divisor is a whole number, write it as a fraction with a denominator of 1.

$3\frac{4}{5} \div 2\frac{3}{4} = \frac{19}{5} \div \frac{11}{4}$

Multiply the dividend by the reciprocal of the divisor. Simplify if possible.

$\frac{19}{5} \div \frac{11}{4} = \frac{19}{5} \times \frac{4}{11} = \frac{19 \times 4}{5 \times 11} = \frac{76}{55} = 1\frac{21}{55}$

**Solve each problem. Simplify if possible.**

A.  $11\frac{1}{2} \div 2\frac{7}{8} =$   $3\frac{1}{2} \div 2 =$   $4\frac{1}{4} \div 3\frac{1}{8} =$

B.  $3\frac{3}{4} \div 5 =$   $3\frac{1}{2} \div 1\frac{3}{4} =$   $6\frac{1}{3} \div 2 =$

C.  $8 \div 1\frac{1}{5} =$   $12\frac{3}{8} \div 2\frac{3}{4} =$   $5\frac{3}{5} \div 4\frac{2}{3} =$

D.  $9 \div 2\frac{5}{8} =$   $7\frac{1}{2} \div 2\frac{1}{2} =$   $1\frac{1}{4} \div 2\frac{1}{2} =$

E.  $7\frac{3}{12} \div 3\frac{1}{2} =$   $7 \div 2\frac{1}{3} =$   $4\frac{1}{6} \div 5 =$

# DIVIDING FRACTIONS PROBLEM SOLVING

**Solve each problem. Simplify if possible.**

A. A box contains 10 ounces of cereal. If one serving is $1\frac{1}{4}$ ounces, how many servings are in the box?

_____

B. A can contains $22\frac{3}{4}$ ounces of soup. If one can contains $3\frac{1}{2}$ servings of soup, how many ounces are in one serving?

_____

C. Ten melons weigh $17\frac{1}{2}$ pounds. What is the average weight of each melon?

_____

D. Christine bought $\frac{3}{4}$ of a pound of grapes to put in her lunches. If she eats the same amount each day and finishes the grapes in 5 days, how much does she eat each day?

_____

E. Mrs. Wilson bought a 35-ounce package of flour. She used $\frac{1}{3}$ of it to bake 5 loaves of bread. How many ounces of flour were in each loaf of bread?

_____

F. Mrs. Gonzalez bought a $2\frac{3}{4}$ pound roast for her family dinner. A total of 9 people will be at the dinner. How much of the roast will each person get if it is divided equally?

_____

# DIVIDING FRACTIONS PROBLEM SOLVING

**Use the information in the box to solve each problem. Simplify if possible.**

> An object on another planet or Earth's moon will weigh a fraction of its weight on Earth. The following chart shows the fraction of an object's Earth weight on some other planets and on Earth's moon.
>
> | Saturn | Mars | Venus | Earth's Moon |
> |--------|------|-------|--------------|
> | $1\frac{1}{5}$ | $\frac{19}{50}$ | $\frac{5}{6}$ | $\frac{1}{6}$ |
>
> **Divide** to find an object's weight on Earth when you know its weight on another planet.
>
> A boulder weighs 950 pounds on Mars. How much would the boulder weigh on Earth?
>
> $\frac{950}{1} \div \frac{19}{50} =$ **2,500 pounds**

A. If a rock weighs 165 pounds on Saturn, how much will it weigh on Earth?

_____

B. An astronaut collected some moon rocks that weighed $12\frac{3}{5}$ pounds on the moon. How much did these moon rocks weigh on Earth?

_____

C. A meteorite weighs 220 pounds on Venus. How much would the meteorite weigh on Earth?

_____

D. If a meteorite weighs $28\frac{1}{2}$ pounds on Mars, how much would it weigh on Earth?

_____

**Write the reciprocal of each number, mixed number, or fraction.**

A.  $\frac{2}{3} =$     $\frac{7}{4} =$     $4\frac{1}{2} =$     $5 =$     $11\frac{1}{3} =$

**Solve each problem. Simplify if possible.**

B.  $4 \div \frac{1}{6} =$     $3 \div \frac{1}{8} =$     $6 \div \frac{1}{5} =$

C.  $5 \div \frac{5}{7} =$     $4 \div \frac{3}{5} =$     $\frac{3}{4} \div \frac{4}{5} =$

D.  $\frac{2}{7} \div \frac{3}{5} =$     $2\frac{2}{3} \div \frac{3}{6} =$     $1\frac{3}{8} \div \frac{2}{4} =$

E.  $\frac{3}{8} \div 3 =$     $\frac{3}{8} \div 2 =$     $3\frac{3}{5} \div 8 =$

F.  $4\frac{3}{9} \div 2\frac{2}{3} =$     $3\frac{6}{8} \div 2\frac{2}{8} =$     $\frac{4}{5} \div \frac{1}{6} =$

**Solve each problem. Simplify if possible.**

G.  Each bead on Josie's necklace is $\frac{3}{4}$ of an inch long. All of the beads together measure $3\frac{3}{4}$ inches. How many beads are part of her necklace?

_____

H.  Kendra bought $\frac{1}{2}$ of a pound of cheese on Monday. For how many days can she eat $\frac{1}{8}$ of a pound of cheese?

_____

**Write the reciprocal of each number, mixed number, or fraction.**

A.   $\dfrac{3}{4} =$          $\dfrac{8}{5} =$          $5\dfrac{1}{3} =$          $7 =$          $10\dfrac{1}{5} =$

**Solve each problem. Simplify if possible.**

B.   $4 \div \dfrac{1}{2} =$          $2 \div \dfrac{1}{10} =$          $3 \div \dfrac{3}{6} =$          $4 \div \dfrac{4}{6} =$

C.   $\dfrac{1}{6} \div \dfrac{2}{6} =$          $\dfrac{2}{3} \div \dfrac{4}{5} =$          $\dfrac{5}{8} \div \dfrac{3}{6} =$          $4\dfrac{1}{2} \div \dfrac{1}{3} =$

D.   $2\dfrac{2}{5} \div \dfrac{2}{3} =$          $\dfrac{3}{4} \div 4 =$          $1\dfrac{1}{16} \div 3 =$          $3\dfrac{3}{5} \div 2 =$

E.   $2 \div 2\dfrac{1}{2} =$          $\dfrac{6}{4} \div 1\dfrac{3}{8} =$          $3\dfrac{4}{9} \div 2\dfrac{1}{9} =$          $\dfrac{8}{5} \div 2\dfrac{2}{5} =$

**Solve each problem. Simplify if possible.**

F.   Dennis wants to form a team to run a relay race. Each team member will need to run $\dfrac{5}{8}$ of a mile. The race is $3\dfrac{3}{4}$ miles. How many runners does Dennis need on his team?

_____

G.   Mrs. Chadwick bought $5\dfrac{1}{2}$ feet of licorice to share equally between her 5 children and herself. How many feet of licorice will each person receive?

_____

# ADDING AND SUBTRACTING DECIMALS

Line up the decimal points. Add or subtract as you would with whole numbers.
Bring the decimal point straight down in the answer.

8.25 + 7.62

$$\begin{array}{r} 8.25 \\ + 7.62 \\ \hline \mathbf{15.87} \end{array}$$

↑
**decimal point**

17.05 – 11.51

$$\begin{array}{r} {}^{6\ 10} \\ 1\cancel{7}.\cancel{0}5 \\ - 11.51 \\ \hline \mathbf{5.54} \end{array}$$

↑
**decimal point**

## Solve each problem.

A.
$$\begin{array}{r} 7.59 \\ + 2.09 \\ \hline \end{array}$$
$$\begin{array}{r} 4.88 \\ + 6.76 \\ \hline \end{array}$$
$$\begin{array}{r} 25.90 \\ + 34.80 \\ \hline \end{array}$$
$$\begin{array}{r} 157.8 \\ + 30.1 \\ \hline \end{array}$$
$$\begin{array}{r} 83.041 \\ + 5.226 \\ \hline \end{array}$$

B.
$$\begin{array}{r} 10.42 \\ - 6.01 \\ \hline \end{array}$$
$$\begin{array}{r} 52.99 \\ - 25.00 \\ \hline \end{array}$$
$$\begin{array}{r} 18.45 \\ - 5.10 \\ \hline \end{array}$$
$$\begin{array}{r} 14.07 \\ - 2.88 \\ \hline \end{array}$$
$$\begin{array}{r} 19.99 \\ - 12.70 \\ \hline \end{array}$$

C.
$$\begin{array}{r} 3.041 \\ 5.226 \\ + 0.451 \\ \hline \end{array}$$
$$\begin{array}{r} 15.08 \\ 46.09 \\ + 145.73 \\ \hline \end{array}$$
$$\begin{array}{r} 35.33 \\ 19.38 \\ + 10.94 \\ \hline \end{array}$$
$$\begin{array}{r} 19.44 \\ - 11.79 \\ \hline \end{array}$$
$$\begin{array}{r} 99.421 \\ - 77.025 \\ \hline \end{array}$$

D.    153.71 + 1.42 =          61.108 + 6.225 =          49.22 + 5.81 + 4.85 =

E.    4.45 – 3.29 =          17.89 – 6.52 =          7.462 – 2.473 =

# ADDING RAGGED DECIMALS

When adding decimals with different place values, write zeros to keep track of the place value columns. Writing zeros to the right of the decimal point does not change the value of the number.

152.6 + 0.765

Line up the decimal points. Write zeros to fill empty place value spaces.

```
  152.600  ←——— Place zeros in the
+   0.765        hundredths and
                 thousandths places.
```

Add as you would with whole numbers. Bring the decimal point straight down in the answer.

```
  152.600
+   0.765
  153.365
```

**Solve each problem.**

A.
```
   0.9          6          8.043        48.643       84.948
+ 0.47      + 7.48       + 3.97        + 6.08       + 37.27
```

B.
```
  36.764       97.4        53.903       69.427       47.67
+ 877.3      + 73.969     + 99.8       + 0.6        + 0.4
```

C.
```
   0.6         24.69         7           28.1         39.48
   0.47         0.104       32.08         7.786       12.2
+ 0.22       + 682.62     + 456.643   + 246.907    + 473.745
```

D.   97.483 + 73.99 =           5.903 + 99.1 =           18.7 + 6.427 =

E.   74.36 + 8.758 =       8.05 + 139.5 + 98.004 =       78 + 746.78 + 9.463 =

## SUBTRACTING RAGGED DECIMALS

When subtracting decimals with different place values, write zeros to regroup between place value columns.

48 – 5.73

Line up the decimal points. Write zeros to fill empty place value spaces.

$$48.\mathbf{00} \longleftarrow$$
$$-\ \ 5.73$$

Add a decimal after the whole number and place **zeros** in the tenths and hundredths places.

Subtract as you would with whole numbers. Bring the decimal point straight down in the answer.

$$48.00$$
$$-\ \ 5.73$$
$$\overline{\mathbf{42.27}}$$

**Solve each problem.**

A.
| 6.2 | 7.2 | 4 | 7 | 6 |
|---|---|---|---|---|
| − 0.76 | − 3.94 | − 1.70 | − 2.85 | − 2.76 |

B.
| 4.54 | 28.4 | 437.1 | 268 | 63.1 |
|---|---|---|---|---|
| − 3 | − 9.63 | − 67.34 | − 168.94 | − 0.099 |

C.
| 20.1 | 47.2 | 70.23 | 64.6 | 42.21 |
|---|---|---|---|---|
| − 0.673 | − 0.499 | − 68 | − 35.072 | − 28 |

D.  25 – 13.75 =          5.3 – 2.148 =          394.2 – 181.004 =

E.  14 – 7.95 =          38 – 27.99 =          365 – 99.559 =

# ADDING AND SUBTRACTING DECIMALS PROBLEM SOLVING

**Solve each problem.**

A. An owner of a retail clothing store bought a dress for $36.25 and sold it for $59.99. What was her profit?

B. A pair of running shoes costs $22.29. The store owner wanted to make a profit of $18.50. What should the selling price be?

C. Malcolm spent $48.74 on new speakers and $25.39 on computer games. After these purchases, he only had $0.58 left. How much money did Malcolm have before he went shopping?

D. Hailey received some money for her birthday. She spent $14.48 on a CD and donated $25.00 to charity. She put half of what was left into her savings account. She has $17.76 left. How much did she receive on her birthday?

E. Keith had $27.00 in his wallet. He bought a movie ticket for $6.25, a box of popcorn for $4.35, and licorice for $2.75. How much money does Keith have left?

F. Wendy spent $13.28 on a scarf and $9.63 on a pair of mittens. After these purchases, she had $25.84 left. How much money did Wendy have before she went shopping?

# ADDING AND SUBTRACTING DECIMALS PROBLEM SOLVING

## Solve each problem.

A. To make the swim team, Pedro must swim 400 meters in less than 7 minutes. Pedro swam the first 200 meters in 2.86 minutes. He swam the second 200 meters in 3.95 minutes. What is the total amount of time he took to swim 400 meters? Did Pedro make the team?

B. The school record for the 400-meter track relay was 65.5 seconds. This year, the Speedsters would like to tie or break the record. It took them 53.96 seconds to run 300 meters. In how much time must they run the last 100 meters to tie the record?

C. The Whiz Kids ran the 400-meter relay in 47.35 seconds. Their time for the first 300 meters was 35.58 seconds. What was their time for the last 100 meters?

D. Jackie won a gymnastics competition. She received a score of 9.2 on the floor exercise, a 9.5 on the vault, a 9.3 on the uneven bars, and an 8.8 on the balance beam. What was Jackie's overall score? If the second-place gymnast's score was 35.7, by how many points did Jackie win?

E. At a track-and-field meet, the winner of the pole vault event cleared a height of 3.25 meters. This was 0.1 meters more than the height cleared by the second-place pole-vaulter. The second-place height was 0.05 meters more than the third-place height. What height did the third-place pole-vaulter clear?

F. Chung noticed a pattern in his long jump distances. So far, they have been 3.2 meters, 3.325 meters, 3.45 meters, and 3.575 meters. Find Chung's pattern. What is the next distance in his pattern?

**Solve each problem.**

A.  $\begin{array}{r} 0.1 \\ + \, 0.08 \\ \hline \end{array}$     $\begin{array}{r} 6.304 \\ + \, 2.180 \\ \hline \end{array}$     $\begin{array}{r} 21.2 \\ 8.406 \\ + \, 40.120 \\ \hline \end{array}$

B.  $\begin{array}{r} 0.26 \\ - \, 0.03 \\ \hline \end{array}$     $\begin{array}{r} 6.461 \\ - \, 0.350 \\ \hline \end{array}$     $\begin{array}{r} 18.269 \\ - \, 3.108 \\ \hline \end{array}$

C.  $\begin{array}{r} 0.48 \\ + \, 0.7 \\ \hline \end{array}$     $\begin{array}{r} 6.783 \\ + \, 9.4 \\ \hline \end{array}$     $\begin{array}{r} 14.16 \\ 9.84 \\ + \, 6.408 \\ \hline \end{array}$

D.  $\begin{array}{r} 0.206 \\ - \, 0.18 \\ \hline \end{array}$     $\begin{array}{r} 6.03 \\ - \, 4.169 \\ \hline \end{array}$     $\begin{array}{r} 24.4 \\ - \, 8.627 \\ \hline \end{array}$

**Solve each problem.**

E.  Cole purchased $115.67 worth of clothing at a department store. The next day, he returned a tie that cost $15.99 and a belt that cost $16.50. He was refunded $1.95 in sales tax. How much did he spend on clothes after returning the tie and the belt?

F.  Tammy swam the length of the pool in 35.6 seconds on Wednesday. This was 1.7 seconds faster than she swam it on Tuesday. What was her time on Tuesday?

# ADDING AND SUBTRACTING DECIMALS ASSESSMENT

**Solve each problem.**

A.
```
   0.6
 + 0.19
```
```
   6.247
 + 3.43
```
```
   24.2
   1.143
 + 3.004
```

B.
```
   0.48
 − 0.07
```
```
   6.043
 − 0.011
```
```
   14.267
 −  3.102
```

C.
```
   0.74
 + 0.6
```
```
   6.764
 + 4.8
```
```
   18.7
   8.69
 + 24.048
```

D.
```
   0.321
 − 0.27
```
```
   5
 − 3.058
```
```
   18.2
 −  9.485
```

**Solve each problem.**

E. Mason spent $74.35 at the music store. The next day, he returned a CD that cost $14.99 and a movie that cost $11.50. He was refunded $1.59 in sales tax. How much did he spend on the items that he kept?

_____

F. Jamie ran around the track in 57.23 seconds on Thursday. This was 2.7 seconds faster than she ran on Wednesday. What was her time on Wednesday?

_____

**MATH SUCCESS** RB-904108

## PLACING DECIMAL POINTS

> To multiply decimals, first multiply as you would with whole numbers. Then, count the total number of decimal places to the right of the decimal point in both factors. That is the number of decimal places in the product.
>
> $\begin{array}{r} 4.69 \\ \times \quad 3 \\ \hline 14.07 \end{array}$ ← **2** decimal places
>  ← + **0** decimal places
>  **2** decimal places
>
> ↑___ **Place decimal point here.**
>
> $\begin{array}{r} 1.54 \\ \times 0.38 \\ \hline 0.5852 \end{array}$ ← **2** decimal places
>  ← + **2** decimal places
>  **4** decimal places
>
> ↑___ **Place decimal point here.**

**Place the decimal point in each answer.**

A.

| 199.6 | 19.96 | 1.996 | 199.6 | 1.996 |
|---|---|---|---|---|
| x    8 | x    8 | x    8 | x   0.8 | x   0.8 |
| 15968 | 15968 | 15968 | 15968 | 15968 |

B.

| 300.4 | 30.04 | 3.004 | 300.4 | 3.004 |
|---|---|---|---|---|
| x    6 | x    6 | x    6 | x   0.6 | x   0.6 |
| 18024 | 18024 | 18024 | 18024 | 18024 |

C.

| 250.2 | 25.02 | 2.502 | 250.2 | 2.502 |
|---|---|---|---|---|
| x    5 | x    5 | x    5 | x   0.5 | x   0.5 |
| 12510 | 12510 | 12510 | 12510 | 12510 |

D.

| 21.7 | 63.1 | 36.6 | 3.41 | 7.67 |
|---|---|---|---|---|
| x 4.2 | x 2.2 | x 4.7 | x 6.2 | x 1.3 |
| 9114 | 13882 | 17202 | 21142 | 9971 |

E.

| 21.43 | 18.72 | 24.062 | 62.003 | 18.417 |
|---|---|---|---|---|
| x 3.04 | x 2.17 | x    1.3 | x    1.4 | x   0.2 |
| 651472 | 406224 | 312806 | 868042 | 36834 |

# MULTIPLYING DECIMALS BY WHOLE NUMBERS

32 x 0.43

Multiply the factors as if the decimal point is not there.

```
    32
  x 0.43
    96
 + 1280
  1376
```

Count the total number of decimal places to the right of the decimal point in both factors. That is the number of decimal places in the product.

```
    32   ←  0 decimal places
  x 0.43 ← + 2 decimal places
    96
 + 1280
  13.76 ←  2 decimal places
```

**Solve each problem.**

A.
```
    0.4        0.9        0.12       4.9
  x   6      x   3      x    7     x   8
```

B.
```
    4.5        2.81       1.76       3.03
  x   3      x    4     x    5     x    6
```

C.
```
    2.8        6.2        3.7        0.17
  x  34      x  13      x  65      x  14
```

D.
```
    0.52       0.208      302.6      3.208
  x   26     x    21    x    83    x    91
```

**MATH SUCCESS** RB-904108

# MULTIPLYING DECIMALS BY DECIMALS

To multiply decimals, first multiply as you would with whole numbers. Then, count the total number of decimal places to the right of the decimal point in both factors. That is the number of decimal places in the product.

1.4 x 0.2

$$
\begin{array}{r}
1.\mathbf{4} \leftarrow \quad \mathbf{1}\ \text{decimal place} \\
\times\ 0.\mathbf{2} \leftarrow \quad +\ \mathbf{1}\ \text{decimal place} \\
\hline
0.\mathbf{28} \leftarrow \quad \mathbf{2}\ \text{decimal places}
\end{array}
$$

2.53 x 3.1

$$
\begin{array}{r}
2.\mathbf{53} \leftarrow \quad \mathbf{2}\ \text{decimal places} \\
\times\ \ \ 3.\mathbf{1} \leftarrow \quad +\ \mathbf{1}\ \text{decimal place} \\
\hline
253 \\
+\ 7590 \\
\hline
7.\mathbf{843} \leftarrow \quad \mathbf{3}\ \text{decimal places}
\end{array}
$$

## Solve each problem.

A.
$$\begin{array}{r} 0.7 \\ \times\ 0.4 \\ \hline \end{array}$$
$$\begin{array}{r} 0.3 \\ \times\ 0.5 \\ \hline \end{array}$$
$$\begin{array}{r} 0.54 \\ \times\ 0.6 \\ \hline \end{array}$$
$$\begin{array}{r} 2.9 \\ \times\ 5.4 \\ \hline \end{array}$$

B.
$$\begin{array}{r} 8.4 \\ \times\ 0.6 \\ \hline \end{array}$$
$$\begin{array}{r} 0.7 \\ \times\ 0.12 \\ \hline \end{array}$$
$$\begin{array}{r} 0.9 \\ \times\ 0.2 \\ \hline \end{array}$$
$$\begin{array}{r} 0.12 \\ \times\ 0.22 \\ \hline \end{array}$$

C.
$$\begin{array}{r} 56.1 \\ \times\ 2.1 \\ \hline \end{array}$$
$$\begin{array}{r} 0.45 \\ \times\ 0.9 \\ \hline \end{array}$$
$$\begin{array}{r} 0.724 \\ \times\ \ \ 0.6 \\ \hline \end{array}$$
$$\begin{array}{r} 0.46 \\ \times\ 0.87 \\ \hline \end{array}$$

D.
$$\begin{array}{r} 4.95 \\ \times\ 0.3 \\ \hline \end{array}$$
$$\begin{array}{r} 0.2 \\ \times\ 7.8 \\ \hline \end{array}$$
$$\begin{array}{r} 9.12 \\ \times\ 4.3 \\ \hline \end{array}$$
$$\begin{array}{r} 10.16 \\ \times\ 2.21 \\ \hline \end{array}$$

# MULTIPLYING DECIMALS WITH ZEROS IN THE PRODUCTS

Sometimes, more decimal places are needed than there are digits in the answer. In this case, add zeros for the additional digits.

1.05 x 0.03

Multiply as you would with whole numbers.

```
     1
   1.05
 x 0.03
   315
```

Count the total number of decimal places. Then, place the decimal point in the answer. Write zeros to fill the extra places.

1.**05** ← **2** decimal places
x 0.**03** ← + **2** decimal places
0.**0**315 ← **4** decimal places needed in answer but only 3 numbers

**Add zero as a placeholder.**

## Solve each problem.

A.
```
   0.091        0.0072        0.0043         0.025
 x 0.02       x   0.07      x    0.9       x 0.04
```

B.
```
   0.0053       0.0048         0.305         0.007
 x   0.33      x   0.14       x 0.008       x 0.45
```

C.
```
   0.165         0.002         0.025         0.057
 x 0.08        x   9.7       x   0.6       x 0.43
```

D.
```
   0.092         0.125        0.0047         0.309
 x 0.086       x 0.023       x   0.83       x 0.09
```

# MULTIPLYING DECIMALS PROBLEM SOLVING

**Solve each problem.**

A. A covered wagon on the Oregon Trail could travel about 2.5 miles per hour on flat terrain. About how many miles could it travel in 9 hours?

B. In 1860, gingham cloth sold for $0.25 per yard. Mrs. Olsen bought 16.4 yards to make clothes for her family. How much did she spend on cloth?

C. In 1863 in Fort Laramie, Wyoming, travelers could buy beef jerky at the trading post for $0.35 per pound. How much would a 16-pound box of jerky cost?

D. In 1838, the Smith family traveled through Ohio by canal in 18.5 hours. The Parley Company of Travelers took 2.3 times as long to go the same distance over land with their wagons. How long did it take the Parley Company?

E. In 1865, pioneer travelers could buy wheat for $0.12 per pound at merchant stops along the Oregon Trail. The Clarks had a barrel that could hold 19.25 pounds of wheat. How much did it cost to fill the barrel?

F. Each wagon in the Parley Company of Travelers wagon train was about 3.65 meters long. If 12 wagons traveled end to end, how long would the wagon train be?

# MULTIPLYING DECIMALS PROBLEM SOLVING

## Use the information to solve each problem.

Mike is in college studying to become a nurse. In many of his laboratory classes, he must measure quantities and record data.

A. Mike performed blood tests using 5 test tubes. Each tube contained 12.73 milliliters of blood. How much blood did he test in all?

_____

B. Mike's lab partner was using a mixture of water and iodine in 8 beakers. Each beaker held 7.012 milliliters of the mixture. How much of the mixture did he have altogether?

_____

C. Mike wrapped a cloth bandage around a patient's arm, wrapping the bandage 15 times before securing it. He used 9.12 centimeters each time he wrapped the bandage. How long was the bandage that he used?

_____

D. In chemistry class, Mike took a package of salt and split the contents evenly into 9 groups. Each group weighed 0.07 kilograms. How much salt was in the original package?

_____

E. In his nutrition class, Mike studied labels on food. According to one candy bar's label, the candy bar contained 12.4 grams of fat. If 1 gram of fat contains 9.4 calories, how many calories from fat are in the candy bar?

_____

F. In biology, Mike viewed a specimen under a microscope. The specimen was 0.021 centimeters wide. The microscope magnified the specimen 100 times larger. How wide did the specimen appear when viewed under the microscope?

_____

**Solve each problem.**

| | | | |
|---|---|---|---|
| A. | 0.09<br>x  23 | 0.8<br>x 0.6 | 0.337<br>x  0.5 | 1.48<br>x 0.36 |

| | | | |
|---|---|---|---|
| B. | 0.03<br>x  0.8 | 0.045<br>x    0.2 | 2.98<br>x 0.05 | 0.003<br>x  7.34 |

| | | | |
|---|---|---|---|
| C. | 0.37<br>x  0.6 | 3.43<br>x  0.6 | 7.4<br>x 5.1 | 0.081<br>x 0.09 |

| | | | |
|---|---|---|---|
| D. | 0.33<br>x  0.2 | 0.034<br>x    6 | 0.063<br>x  0.82 | 2.621<br>x  0.35 |

**Solve each problem.**

E.  A tube of toothpaste holds 6.4 ounces. How much toothpaste do 13 tubes hold?

_____

F.  Keith buys 2.4 pounds of apples at $0.90 per pound. How much does Keith spend on apples?

_____

**Solve each problem.**

A.
$$\begin{array}{r} 0.07 \\ \times\ 18 \\ \hline \end{array}$$
$$\begin{array}{r} 0.7 \\ \times 0.6 \\ \hline \end{array}$$
$$\begin{array}{r} 0.258 \\ \times\ 0.4 \\ \hline \end{array}$$
$$\begin{array}{r} 3.14 \\ \times 0.86 \\ \hline \end{array}$$

B.
$$\begin{array}{r} 0.07 \\ \times\ 0.9 \\ \hline \end{array}$$
$$\begin{array}{r} 0.075 \\ \times\ 0.4 \\ \hline \end{array}$$
$$\begin{array}{r} 2.87 \\ \times 0.05 \\ \hline \end{array}$$
$$\begin{array}{r} 0.003 \\ \times 9.26 \\ \hline \end{array}$$

C.
$$\begin{array}{r} 0.27 \\ \times\ 0.9 \\ \hline \end{array}$$
$$\begin{array}{r} 2.54 \\ \times\ 0.7 \\ \hline \end{array}$$
$$\begin{array}{r} 8.3 \\ \times 9.2 \\ \hline \end{array}$$
$$\begin{array}{r} 0.062 \\ \times\ 0.03 \\ \hline \end{array}$$

D.
$$\begin{array}{r} 6.345 \\ \times\ 0.07 \\ \hline \end{array}$$
$$\begin{array}{r} 1.75 \\ \times 0.06 \\ \hline \end{array}$$
$$\begin{array}{r} 0.098 \\ \times\ 0.55 \\ \hline \end{array}$$
$$\begin{array}{r} 2.263 \\ \times\ 0.04 \\ \hline \end{array}$$

**Solve each problem.**

E. A machine part weighs 1.34 ounces. How much do 50 of the same part weigh?

F. In the turtle trot race, a turtle travels at a rate of 0.09 miles per hour. How far will the turtle travel in 0.40 hours?

# DIVIDING DECIMALS BY WHOLE NUMBERS

$3.25 \div 5$

Place the decimal point in the quotient directly above the decimal point in the dividend.

$$5\overline{)3.25}$$

**Remember:** The dividend is the number that will be divided.

Divide as you would for whole numbers.

```
    0.65
5)3.25
  - 3 0
    25
  - 25
     0
```

Check by multiplying.

```
  0.65
x    5
 3.25
```

**Solve each problem.**

A.  $8\overline{)2.4}$          $8\overline{)0.24}$          $3\overline{)0.69}$          $3\overline{)0.069}$

B.  $2\overline{)45.4}$          $2\overline{)4.54}$          $7\overline{)34.37}$          $5\overline{)0.105}$

C.  $6\overline{)120.6}$          $6\overline{)12.06}$          $4\overline{)2.44}$          $6\overline{)2.76}$

D.  $6\overline{)5.88}$          $4\overline{)7.36}$          $8\overline{)7.592}$          $8\overline{)10.40}$

## ZEROS IN THE DIVIDENDS

When dividing decimals, instead of writing a remainder, you can add zeros to the dividend to keep dividing until the remainder is zero.

$2.5 \div 4$

Place the decimal point in the quotient directly above the decimal point in the dividend. Then, divide the tenths.

$$
\begin{array}{r}
0.\mathbf{6} \\
4\overline{)2.5} \\
-\ 2\ 4 \\
\hline
\mathbf{I} \leftarrow \text{remainder}
\end{array}
$$

Write a zero in the hundredths place of the dividend.

$$
\begin{array}{r}
0.6\mathbf{2} \\
4\overline{)2.5\mathbf{0}} \leftarrow \text{Write a} \\
-\ 2\ 4\!\downarrow \quad \text{zero here.} \\
\hline
\mathbf{10} \leftarrow \text{Bring down the} \\
-\ \mathbf{8} \quad \text{zero. Divide by 4.} \\
\hline
\mathbf{2} \\
\uparrow \\
\text{remainder}
\end{array}
$$

Write a zero in the thousandths place of the dividend. Bring down the zero and divide.

$$
\begin{array}{r}
0.62\mathbf{5} \\
4\overline{)2.50\mathbf{0}} \leftarrow \text{Write a} \\
-\ 2\ 4 \quad \text{zero here.} \\
\hline
10 \\
-\ 8\!\downarrow \\
\hline
\mathbf{20} \leftarrow \text{Bring down the} \\
-\ \mathbf{20} \quad \text{zero. Divide by 4.} \\
\hline
\mathbf{0} \leftarrow \text{no remainder}
\end{array}
$$

**Solve each problem.**

A.  $5\overline{)2.7}$      $4\overline{)4.6}$      $6\overline{)5.7}$      $4\overline{)7.3}$      $8\overline{)2.5}$

B.  $5\overline{)8.1}$      $4\overline{)6.3}$      $4\overline{)4.2}$      $5\overline{)4.19}$      $5\overline{)3.74}$

C.  $4\overline{)53.4}$      $18\overline{)9.63}$      $40\overline{)53.6}$      $16\overline{)5.2}$      $56\overline{)9.8}$

**MATH SUCCESS** RB-904108      © Rainbow Bridge Publishing

## ZEROS IN THE QUOTIENTS

$0.192 \div 32$

| Place the decimal point in the quotient directly above the decimal point in the dividend. | Divide. You cannot divide 1 by 32. Write a zero in the quotient. | You cannot divide 19 by 32. Write another zero in the quotient. | Divide 192 by 32. |
|---|---|---|---|
| $\overset{.}{32)\overline{0.192}}$ | $\overset{0.0}{32)\overline{0.192}}$ | $\overset{0.00}{32)\overline{0.192}}$ | $\begin{array}{r} 0.00\mathbf{6} \\ 32)\overline{0.192} \\ -192 \\ \hline 0 \end{array}$ |

**Solve each problem.**

A.  $7)\overline{0.56}$      $2)\overline{0.018}$      $3)\overline{0.21}$      $6)\overline{0.096}$      $8)\overline{0.52}$

B.  $8)\overline{0.19}$      $5)\overline{0.451}$      $6)\overline{0.1065}$      $4)\overline{0.38}$      $24)\overline{0.15}$

C.  $65)\overline{1.95}$      $29)\overline{0.174}$      $71)\overline{0.923}$      $12)\overline{0.42}$      $59)\overline{1.947}$

## DIVIDING DECIMALS BY DECIMALS

To divide by a decimal, you must move the decimal point to make the divisor a whole number.

$5.44 \div 1.6$

Move the decimal point one place to the right to make the divisor a whole number. Move the decimal point in the dividend the same number of places.

$1.6\overline{)5.44} \longrightarrow 16\overline{)54.4}$

Divide as you would with whole numbers.

$$\begin{array}{r} 3.4 \\ 16\overline{)54.4} \\ -48 \phantom{.4} \\ \hline 64 \\ -64 \\ \hline 0 \end{array}$$

**Solve each problem.**

A.  $0.6\overline{)5.4}$         $0.9\overline{)0.18}$         $1.4\overline{)13.86}$         $0.86\overline{)0.688}$

B.  $1.7\overline{)10.54}$         $2.4\overline{)16.8}$         $0.07\overline{)0.035}$         $0.92\overline{)0.736}$

C.  $0.005\overline{)0.015}$         $3.2\overline{)13.76}$         $0.63\overline{)0.441}$         $0.086\overline{)0.0258}$

D.  $0.4\overline{)0.856}$         $2.8\overline{)2.716}$         $0.37\overline{)0.3108}$         $0.65\overline{)0.1105}$

# DIVIDING DECIMALS PROBLEM SOLVING

When finding a unit cost, divide the total cost by the number of units.

**Total Cost ÷ Number of Units = Unit Cost**

Maria bought a **15**-ounce bag of tortilla chips for **$2.25**. What is the cost per ounce?

$ 0.15 ← **Unit Cost (per ounce)**

**Number** → 15)$2.25 ← **Total Cost**
**of Units**
　　　　　　　−15
　　　　　　　　75
　　　　　　　−75
　　　　　　　　　0

The tortilla chips cost $0.15 per ounce.

## Solve each problem.

A.   At Orchard Street Market, 4.5 pounds of pears cost $2.97. What is the cost per pound?

B.   Mrs. Parks bought 30 ice cream bars for her daughter's class party. She paid $12.60. How much did each ice cream bar cost?

C.   Sandy bought a 32.5-ounce package of mixed nuts for $7.15. What was the cost per ounce?

D.   A $2.56 can of lemonade mix will make 64 cups of lemonade. What is the cost per cup?

E.   Whole watermelons are sold for $3.99 each. Sonia bought a watermelon that weighed 21 pounds. What price per pound did she pay?

F.   Shawn bought 8 pounds of apples for $10.32. How much did he pay per pound?

# DIVIDING DECIMALS PROBLEM SOLVING

## Use the table to solve each problem.

Did you know that sound energy can be measured in watts? This table shows the energy output of some musical instruments.

| Instrument | Energy Output |
|------------|---------------|
| piano | 0.44 watt |
| trombone | 6.4 watts |
| snare drum | 12.3 watts |

How many snare drums would it take to produce 73.8 watts of energy?
**Think:** 73.8 ÷ 12.3

$$12.3\overline{)73.8} \longrightarrow \overset{\textbf{6 snare drums}}{123\overline{)738}}$$
$$-738$$
$$0$$

A. How many trombones would it take to produce 1,280 watts of energy?

B. A piano can produce 8 times as much sound energy as a flute. How much energy does a flute produce?

C. About how many pianos playing together will produce the same sound energy as one snare drum? (Hint: You cannot have part of a piano playing. Round the remainder to the nearest whole number.)

D. A trombone can produce 80 times as much sound energy as a piccolo. What is the energy of a piccolo?

**MATH SUCCESS** RB-904108

# DIVIDING DECIMALS ASSESSMENT

**Solve each problem.**

A. $8\overline{)7.2}$ $18\overline{)7.56}$ $6\overline{)1.38}$ $35\overline{)74.9}$

B. $4\overline{)32.12}$ $14\overline{)70.98}$ $36\overline{)0.324}$ $58\overline{)0.3654}$

C. $0.6\overline{)0.048}$ $0.56\overline{)1.288}$ $0.8\overline{)184}$ $0.25\overline{)9}$

D. $3.5\overline{)59.5}$ $0.2\overline{)4.18}$ $0.003\overline{)93.6}$ $0.004\overline{)0.624}$

**Solve each problem.**

E. An 11-ounce bottle of shampoo costs $2.97. What is the cost per ounce?

____________________

F. A 12-story building is 127.2 feet tall. How tall is each story if they are all the same height?

____________________

**Solve each problem.**

A.  $9\overline{)5.4}$        $12\overline{)4.44}$        $7\overline{)0.84}$        $52\overline{)71.24}$

B.  $8\overline{)40.72}$        $13\overline{)26.39}$        $48\overline{)0.144}$        $43\overline{)0.1591}$

C.  $0.7\overline{)0.028}$        $0.43\overline{)0.645}$        $0.4\overline{)72}$        $0.16\overline{)4}$

D.  $0.72\overline{)3.6}$        $0.6\overline{)261}$        $0.002\overline{)0.06}$        $0.51\overline{)163.2}$

**Solve each problem.**

E.  Jason spent $12.25 on a pack of trading cards. If the pack contains 25 cards, what is the cost per card?

F.  A marble factory uses 586.5 grams of glass to make 75 marbles of the same size. How much does each marble weigh?

**MATH SUCCESS** RB-904108                © Rainbow Bridge Publishing

## CHANGING FRACTIONS TO DECIMALS

To write a fraction as a decimal, divide the numerator by the denominator.

$\frac{5}{8} = 5 \div 8$

$$\begin{array}{r} 0.625 \\ 8\overline{)5.000} \\ -48 \\ \hline 20 \\ -16 \\ \hline 40 \\ -40 \\ \hline 0 \end{array}$$

← Remember that you may need to add zeros to finish the division.

**Write each fraction as a decimal.**

A. $\frac{4}{5} =$ $\qquad$ $\frac{3}{8} =$ $\qquad$ $\frac{3}{5} =$ $\qquad$ $\frac{9}{15} =$ $\qquad$ $\frac{19}{25} =$

B. $\frac{17}{20} =$ $\qquad$ $\frac{1}{25} =$ $\qquad$ $\frac{9}{40} =$ $\qquad$ $\frac{18}{25} =$ $\qquad$ $\frac{3}{16} =$

C. $\frac{111}{200} =$ $\qquad$ $\frac{5}{16} =$ $\qquad$ $\frac{45}{200} =$ $\qquad$ $\frac{8}{25} =$ $\qquad$ $\frac{19}{40} =$

D. $\frac{9}{12} =$ $\qquad$ $\frac{11}{16} =$ $\qquad$ $\frac{4}{8} =$ $\qquad$ $\frac{87}{200} =$ $\qquad$ $\frac{3}{25} =$

# CHANGING DECIMALS TO FRACTIONS

When writing a decimal as a fraction, the digits to the right of the decimal point become the numerator. The denominator is determined by the place value of the numbers to the right of the decimal point.

**0.15**

0.15 is the same as saying "15 hundredths" or "15 over 100."

$0.15 = \dfrac{15}{100}$

Simplify if possible.

$\dfrac{15}{100} = \mathbf{\dfrac{3}{20}}$

**5.6**

5.6 is the same as saying "5 and 6 tenths" or "5 and 6 over 10."

$5.6 = 5\dfrac{6}{10}$

Simplify if possible.

$5\dfrac{6}{10} = \mathbf{5\dfrac{3}{5}}$

**0.064**

0.064 is the same as saying "64 thousandths" or "64 over 1,000."

$0.064 = \dfrac{64}{1,000}$

Simplify if possible.

$\dfrac{64}{1,000} = \mathbf{\dfrac{8}{125}}$

**Write each decimal as a fraction or a mixed number. Simplify if possible.**

A.  0.1 =            2.6 =            0.4 =            6.5 =

B.  8.7 =            0.9 =            4.8 =            0.3 =

C.  0.20 =           0.25 =           0.55 =           6.34 =

D.  8.08 =           0.04 =           0.01 =           4.06 =

E.  0.42 =           1.75 =           0.488 =          0.86 =

F.  2.500 =          0.505 =          3.404 =          0.532 =

G.  7.266 =          0.275 =          9.454 =          0.844 =

 **MATH SUCCESS** RB-904108

# CHANGING FRACTIONS TO PERCENTS AND PERCENTS TO FRACTIONS

The number 100 is used in ratios called **percents**. Percent means "per 100."

The grid contains 100 squares. 75 of the 100 squares are shaded.

As a fraction, the shaded part is $\frac{75}{100}$ (or $\frac{3}{4}$ in simplest form).

To change a fraction to a percent, convert a fraction in simplest form to a fraction with a denominator of 100.

$$\frac{3}{4} = \frac{n}{100}$$

Multiply the numerator and the denominator by 25.

$$\frac{3 \times 25}{4 \times 25} = \frac{75}{100}$$

$n = 75$. Once you have solved for the numerator, add a percent sign (%) after it. Delete the denominator. As a percent, the shaded part is 75%.

$$\frac{3}{4} = \frac{75}{100} = \mathbf{75\%}$$

To change a percent to a fraction, write the percent over 100. Delete the percent sign. Then, simplify the fraction if possible.

$$75\% = \frac{75}{100} = \mathbf{\frac{3}{4}}$$

**Write each fraction as a percent.**

A.    $\frac{9}{100} =$          $\frac{1}{25} =$          $\frac{3}{10} =$          $\frac{1}{2} =$

B.    $\frac{4}{5} =$          $\frac{1}{10} =$          $\frac{2}{2} =$          $\frac{7}{50} =$

**Write each percent as a fraction with 100 as the denominator and as a fraction in lowest terms.**

| Percent | 25% | 3% | 50% | 33% | 65% | 56% | 30% | 5% | 98% | 7% |
|---|---|---|---|---|---|---|---|---|---|---|
| Equivalent Ratio | $\frac{25}{100}$ | $\frac{3}{100}$ | | | | | | | | |
| Fraction in Lowest Terms | $\frac{1}{4}$ | $\frac{3}{100}$ | | | | | | | | |

# CHANGING FRACTIONS TO PERCENTS AND PERCENTS TO FRACTIONS

**Write each fraction as a percent.**

A.  $\dfrac{3}{4} =$  $\dfrac{1}{4} =$  $\dfrac{1}{2} =$  $\dfrac{1}{10} =$

B.  $\dfrac{11}{100} =$  $\dfrac{73}{100} =$  $\dfrac{1}{5} =$  $\dfrac{1}{20} =$

C.  $\dfrac{3}{5} =$  $\dfrac{9}{10} =$  $\dfrac{13}{100} =$  $\dfrac{89}{100} =$

**Write each percent as a fraction in lowest terms.**

D.  4% =  16% =  25% =  34% =

E.  75% =  15% =  20% =  13% =

F.  18% =  64% =  70% =  10% =

**MATH SUCCESS** RB-904108

## PERCENTS AS DECIMALS

To change a **decimal to a percent**, multiply by 100. Then, write a percent sign (%).

0.36 x 100 = **36%**          0.04 x 100 = **4%**          0.152 x 100 = **15.2%**

Or, you may use place value to determine the answer. Multiplying by 100 is the same as moving the decimal point 2 places to the right. Move the decimal point two places to the right. Then, add the percent sign (%).

0.36 = **36%**          0.04 = **4%**          0.152 = **15.2%**

To change a **percent to a decimal**, divide the percent by 100 and delete the percent sign.

42% ÷ 100 = **0.42**          9% ÷ 100 = **0.09**          23.5% ÷ 100 = **0.235**

Or, you may use place value to determine the answer. Dividing by 100 is the same as moving the decimal point 2 places to the left.

42% = **0.42**          9% = **0.09**          23.5% = **0.235**

**Write each decimal as a percent.**

A.    0.02 =          0.06 =          0.01 =          0.12 =

B.    0.37 =          0.69 =          0.40 =          0.21 =

C.    0.999 =          0.499 =          1.75 =          2.25 =

**Write each percent as a decimal.**

D.    24% =          65% =          88% =          3% =

E.    17% =          9% =          10% =          86% =

F.    66.7% =          33.3% =          145% =          210% =

# FINDING PERCENTS OF NUMBERS

To find a percent of a number, multiply by either an equivalent fraction or an equivalent decimal.

Find **20% of 130**.
Convert the percent and the number to fractions. Multiply.

20% of 130 = 20% x 130

$20\% = \dfrac{20}{100} = \dfrac{1}{5}$

$\dfrac{1}{5} \times \dfrac{130}{1} = \dfrac{130}{5}$

Simplify.

$\dfrac{130}{5} = \textbf{26}$

20% of 130 is **26**.

Find **4% of 25**.
Convert the percent to a decimal. Multiply.

4% of 25 = 0.04 x 25

$$\begin{array}{r} \overset{2}{0.0}4 \\ \times\ \ 25 \\ \hline 020 \\ +\ 0080 \\ \hline 01.00 = \textbf{1.00 or 1} \end{array}$$

4% of 25 is **1**.

**Find the percent of each number using either method shown.**

A.   3% of 10 =                 4% of 30 =                 16% of 80 =

B.   18% of 36 =                6% of 80 =                 9% of 90 =

C.   8% of 68 =                 9% of 75 =                 62% of 62 =

D.   4% of 400 =               3% of 200 =                37% of 51 =

E.   1% of 246 =               5% of 286 =                60% of 300 =

**MATH SUCCESS** RB-904108

# FINDING DISCOUNTS AND SALE PRICES

A **discount** is an amount decreased from a regular price. A discounted price is often called a **sale price**.

A camera is discounted 40%. Its regular price is $250.00. Find the discount amount and the sale price for the camera.

**discount = regular price x discount rate**
  = $250 x 40%
  = $250 x 0.4
  = **$100**

**sale price = regular price – discount**
  = $250 – $100
  = **$150**

**Complete the table.**

|   | Regular Price | Discount Rate | Discount | Sale Price |
|---|---|---|---|---|
| A. | $24 | 40% | | |
| B. | $25 | 30% | | |
| C. | $80 | 15% | | |
| D. | $220 | 60% | | |
| E. | $90 | 55% | | |
| F. | $120 | 45% | | |
| G. | $1,250 | 25% | | |
| H. | $198 | 50% | | |
| I. | $65 | 15% | | |
| J. | $4 | 40% | | |
| K. | $80 | 10% | | |
| L. | $20 | 35% | | |
| M. | $6 | 20% | | |
| N. | $99 | 33% | | |

# NUMBER PATTERNS

A **number pattern** is a list of numbers that occur in a predictable way. Many patterns use addition and subtraction. To find the pattern, write the number that you need to add or subtract to find the next number in the pattern.

Find the next three numbers in this pattern: **1, 7, 2, 8, 3, 9, 4, \_\_\_, \_\_\_, \_\_\_**

Determine the pattern by writing the number you must add or subtract to get the next number.

The pattern is **add 6, subtract 5**.

Use the pattern to calculate the next three numbers.

$$4 + \mathbf{6} = \mathbf{10}$$
$$10 - \mathbf{5} = \mathbf{5}$$
$$5 + \mathbf{6} = \mathbf{11}$$

The next three numbers in the pattern are **10, 5, and 11**.

**Find the next three numbers in each number pattern.**

A.    5, 8, 11, 14, 17, \_\_\_, \_\_\_, \_\_\_

B.    91, 86, 81, 76, 71, \_\_\_, \_\_\_, \_\_\_

C.    100, 92, 84, 76, 68, \_\_\_, \_\_\_, \_\_\_

D.    10, 20, 25, 35, 40, \_\_\_, \_\_\_, \_\_\_

E.    72, 69, 66, 63, 60, \_\_\_, \_\_\_, \_\_\_

F.    317, 402, 487, 572, \_\_\_, \_\_\_, \_\_\_

G.    5, 11, 23, 41, 65, \_\_\_, \_\_\_, \_\_\_

H.    244, 226, 208, 190, \_\_\_, \_\_\_, \_\_\_

I.    1, 4, 9, 16, 25, \_\_\_, \_\_\_, \_\_\_

J.    1, 2, 4, 8, 16, \_\_\_, \_\_\_, \_\_\_

K.    53, 54, 56, 59, 63, \_\_\_, \_\_\_, \_\_\_

L.    30, 34, 40, 48, 58, \_\_\_, \_\_\_, \_\_\_

M.    11, 16, 14, 19, 17, \_\_\_, \_\_\_, \_\_\_

N.    19, 34, 49, 64, 79, \_\_\_, \_\_\_, \_\_\_

 **MATH SUCCESS** RB-904108     

# FUNCTIONS AND PATTERNS

The figures below are models of buildings made with blocks. Notice the pattern that relates the number of blocks in each tower and the total number of blocks used in the building.

The building with **1** block for its tower takes **6** blocks to build.

The building with **2** blocks for its tower takes **7** blocks to build.

The building with **3** blocks for its tower takes **8** blocks to build.

Look at the table and the statement that gives the general rule for the pattern.

| Number of Blocks in Tower | 1 | 2 | 3 | 4 | 10 | 20 |
|---|---|---|---|---|---|---|
| Number of Blocks in Entire Building | 6 | 7 | 8 | 9 | 15 | 25 |

The pattern is:      **+5**   **+5**   **+5**   **+5**   **+5**   **+5**

To find the number of blocks in each building, **add five** to the number of blocks in the tower.

**Complete each table. Then, fill in the statement that gives the general rule for the pattern.**

A.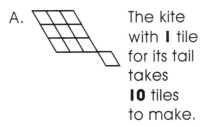
The kite with **1** tile for its tail takes **10** tiles to make.

The kite with **2** tiles for its tail takes **11** tiles to make.

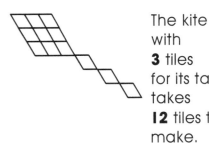
The kite with **3** tiles for its tail takes **12** tiles to make.

| Number of Tiles in Tail | 1 | 2 | 3 | 4 | 10 | 20 |
|---|---|---|---|---|---|---|
| Number of Tiles in Entire Kite | 10 | 11 | 12 | | | |

To find the number of tiles in the kite, _____ to the number of tiles in the tail.

# FUNCTIONS AND PATTERNS

**Complete each table. Then, fill in the statement that gives the general rule for the pattern.**

A.

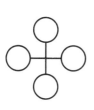     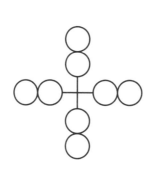     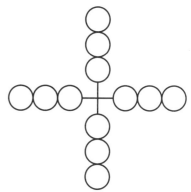

| The design with **1** circle extending on each branch is made with **4** circles. | The design with **2** circles extending on each branch is made with **8** circles. | The design with **3** circles extending on each branch is made with **12** circles. |

| Number of Circles on Each Branch | 1 | 2 | 3 | 4 | 10 | 20 |
|---|---|---|---|---|---|---|
| Number of Circles in Entire Design | 4 | 8 | 12 | | | |

To find the number of circles in the design, _____ the number of circles

on each branch by _____ .

B.

The "chair" that is **2** blocks tall takes **3** blocks to build.   The "chair" that is **3** blocks tall takes **5** blocks to build.   The "chair" that is **4** blocks tall takes **7** blocks to build.

| Height of "Chair" in Blocks | 2 | 3 | 4 | 5 | 6 | 10 | 100 |
|---|---|---|---|---|---|---|---|
| Number of Blocks in Entire "Chair" | 3 | 5 | 7 | | | | |

To find the number of blocks in a "chair," multiply the number of blocks in the "chair's"

height by _____ and subtract _____ .

**MATH SUCCESS** RB-904108                    © Rainbow Bridge Publishing

## TABLES

Write a method for calculating *y* if you know *x*. Then, complete the table.

| x | y |
|---|---|
| 0 | 2 |
| 1 | 3 |
| 2 | 4 |
| 3 | 5 |
| 4 |   |
| 8 |   |

To get from 0 to 2, **add 2**.
To get from 1 to 3, **add 2**.
To get from 2 to 4, **add 2**.
To get from 3 to 5, **add 2**.

rule: **y = x + 2**

For x = 4, y = 4 + 2 = **6**.
For x = 8, y = 8 + 2 = **10**.

Sometimes, a dot (•) is used in math problems as a symbol for "multiply."

In the following table, *y* is 2 times *x*. The rule for finding *y* is to multiply *x* by 2, or **y = 2 · x**.

| x | 0 | 1 | 2 | 3 |
|---|---|---|---|---|
| y | 0 | 2 | 4 | 6 |

**Find the rule for calculating y. Then, complete each table.**

A.

| x | 1 | 3 | 5 | 7 | 9 | 11 |
|---|---|---|---|---|---|----|
| y | 5 | 7 | 9 |   |   |    |

rule: _____

B.

| x | 6 | 7 | 8 | 9 | 10 | 11 |
|---|---|---|---|---|----|----|
| y | 4 | 5 | 6 |   |    |    |

rule: _____

C.

| x | 3  | 4  | 5  | 6 | 7 | 8 |
|---|----|----|----|---|---|---|
| y | 12 | 16 | 20 |   |   |   |

rule: _____

D.

| x | 2 | 4  | 6  | 8 | 10 | 12 |
|---|---|----|----|---|----|----|
| y | 6 | 12 | 18 |   |    |    |

rule: _____

E.

| x | 6 | 8 | 10 | 12 | 14 | 16 |
|---|---|---|----|----|----|----|
| y | 3 | 4 | 5  |    |    |    |

rule: _____

F.

| x | 3 | 7 | 8 | 5 | 10 | 21 |
|---|---|---|---|---|----|----|
| y | 2 | 6 | 7 |   |    |    |

rule: _____

G.

| x | 2  | 3  | 4  | 5 | 6 | 7 |
|---|----|----|----|---|---|---|
| y | 17 | 18 | 19 |   |   |   |

rule: _____

H.

| x | 10 | 11 | 12 | 13 | 14 | 15 |
|---|----|----|----|----|----|----|
| y | 20 | 22 | 24 |    |    |    |

rule: _____

# SOLVING FOR VARIABLES

An algebraic equation contains numbers, **variables**, operations, and an equal sign. A variable is a letter that stands for an unknown number. In the equation $x + 3 = 10$, $x$ is the variable and **+** is the operation. This equation means that some number ($x$) plus 3 is equal to 10. To solve for the variable, use the **inverse**, or opposite, operation.

$x + 3 = 10$

**Think:** What number plus 3 is equal to 10?     $x + 3 = 10$

Choose the inverse operation. Because it is an addition problem, subtract 3 from both sides of the equation.

$x + 3 - 3 = 10 - 3$
$x = 10 - 3$

Simplify.

$x = 7$

Check your solution. Substitute 7 for $x$ in the original equation to see if the equation is true.

$7 + 3 = 10$
$10 = 10$
The equation is true. The solution is correct.

**Solve each equation.**

A.  $x + 8 = 12$          $a + 7 = 18$          $z + 6 = 14$
    $x = 12 - $\_\_\_\_      $a = 18 - $\_\_\_\_      $z = 14 - $\_\_\_\_
    $x = $\_\_\_\_           $a = $\_\_\_\_           $z = $\_\_\_\_

**Solve each equation.**

B.   $y + 8 = 11$     $x + 8 = 24$     $v + 3 = 13$     $m + 12 = 18$

C.   $q - 15 = 100$     $r - 19 = 37$     $w - 32 = 32$     $z - 12 = 29$

D.   $a + 7 = 20$     $y - 22 = 45$     $g + 15 = 31$     $c - 83 = 24$

# SOLVING FOR VARIABLES

Use **inverse operations** to solve multiplication and division equations. The fraction bar is also a division bar: $n/8$ is the same as $n \div 8$.

**Think:** What number times 6 is equal to 54?

$6 \cdot y = 54$

Choose the inverse operation. Divide both sides of the equation by 6.

$$\frac{6 \cdot y}{6} = \frac{54}{6}$$

$$\frac{6}{6} = 1, \text{ so } \frac{6 \cdot y}{6} = 1y = y$$

Simplify.

$y = 54 \div \mathbf{6}$

Check your solution. Substitute 9 for $y$ in the original equation to see if the equation is true.

**$y = 9$**

$6 \cdot 9 = 54$
$54 = 54$
The equation is true. The solution is correct.

**Solve each equation.**

A.    $t \cdot 8 = 72$            $81 \div n = 81$           $y \cdot 6 = 42$

       $t = 72 \div 8$           $n = 81 \cdot$ _____      $y = 42 \div$ _____

       $t =$ _____             $n =$ _____           $y =$ _____

B.    $x \cdot 3 = 12$          $v \cdot 6 = 24$          $h \cdot 8 = 64$          $g \cdot 9 = 27$

C.    $c/5 = 10$            $g \div 4 = 9$          $y/25 = 75$         $s \div 22 = 11$

D.    $b \cdot 7 = 28$          $f \cdot 3 = 51$          $d/82 = 6$           $z/29 = 16$

# PROBABILITY

Probability tells how likely it is that something will happen. It can be written as a fraction.

Determine the probability of the spinner landing on a yellow space.

$$P(\text{yellow}) = \frac{\text{Number of Yellow Spaces}}{\text{Number of Total Spaces}} = \frac{1}{4} = \frac{\text{Favorable Outcomes (Chances)}}{\text{Possible Outcomes (Possibilities)}}$$

The probability that the spinner will land on yellow is $\frac{1}{4}$.
(Read as "one in four.")

For red, P(red) = Number of Red Spaces/Number of Total Spaces

Probability = $\frac{2}{4} = \frac{1}{2}$.

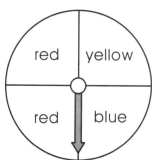

The probability that the spinner will land on red is $\frac{1}{2}$, or one in two.

**Use the information to determine the probability of each event happening. Simplify if possible.**

A jar contains 18 marbles that are all the same size. It contains 7 purple marbles, 3 green marbles, and 8 orange marbles. Without looking, Travis picks 1 marble. What is the probability of each of the following outcomes?

A.   P(green) = $\frac{3}{18}$ = $\frac{1}{6}$      P(purple) =           P(orange) =

B.   P(not green) =        P(purple or green) =      P(not orange) =

**Use the information to determine the probability of each event happening. Simplify if possible.**

A die numbered 1 through 6 is rolled. Find the probability of rolling each outcome.

C.   P(5) =           P(1 or 2) =          P(odd number) =

D.   P(not 6) =        P(even number) =     P(1, 2, 3, or 4) =

# MEAN, MEDIAN, MODE, AND RANGE

Various statistics can be found using a certain data set, including the mean, median, mode, and range.

Distances covered by Run-for-Your-Health participants: 5 miles, 8 miles, 3 miles, 1 mile, 3 miles

The **mean** (or **average**) is the sum of the items divided by the number of items.

$$\frac{5 + 8 + 3 + 1 + 3}{5}$$

$$= \frac{20}{5} = \textbf{4 miles}$$

The **median** is the middle number when the data are arranged from least to greatest.

1   3   **3**   5   8

**median**

If there are two middle numbers, use the average of the two.

The **mode** is the number that occurs most frequently.

1   **3**   **3**   5   8

**mode**

A data set can have more than one mode. However, if no number occurs more frequently than the others, the data set has no mode.

The **range** is the difference between the greatest value (**8**) and the lowest value (**1**) in the data.

**8 – 1 = 7 miles**

**Find the mean, median, mode, and range of each set of data.**

A.  34, 41, 33, 41, 31

mean: _____        median: _____

mode: _____        range: _____

B.  18, 10, 10, 8, 35, 10, 21

mean: _____        median: _____

mode: _____        range: _____

C.  7, 14, 10, 14, 29, 16, 15

mean: _____        median: _____

mode: _____        range: _____

D.  41, 18, 24, 41, 72, 82, 16

mean: _____        median: _____

mode: _____        range: _____

## MAKING PREDICTIONS FROM SAMPLES

A **sample** is a small set or group taken from a large set or population group. **Predictions** can be made about the large group by looking at the sample group.

Cody had a box with **200** marbles in it. The marbles are red, green, yellow, and blue. Without looking, Cody randomly took **20** marbles out of the box. In this sample, **8** of the marbles were red. Approximately how many red marbles should Cody predict are in the box?

Write a proportion in the form of equivalent fractions.

red marbles in sample $\longrightarrow$ $\dfrac{8}{20} = \dfrac{n}{200}$ $\longleftarrow$ red marbles in box
total marbles in sample $\longrightarrow$ $\phantom{\dfrac{8}{20}}$ $\longleftarrow$ total marbles in box

Use equivalent fractions to solve.

$\dfrac{8 \times 10}{20 \times 10} = \dfrac{\mathbf{80}}{200}$  Cody should predict that there are approximately **80** red marbles in the box of 200 marbles.

**Solve each problem.**

A. In a sample, 11 out of 25 marbles are green. Predict approximately how many green marbles are in a box of 100 marbles.

B. In a sample, 54 out of 75 middle school students said that they planned to go to the school carnival. Based on this sample, approximately how many of the 750 middle school students would you predict will go to the carnival?

C. In a sample of 50 sixth-grade students, 32 students said that they are entering the school writing contest. Based on this sample, approximately how many of the 250 sixth graders would you predict will enter the writing contest?

D. A representative sample of T-shirt sizes of 25 sixth graders was taken. The results were: small–3, medium–9, large–13. Predict approximately how many of each size should be ordered for the 250 students in the sixth grade.

**MATH SUCCESS** RB-904108

# WRITING RATIOS

A **ratio** is a comparison of two numbers. One way to write a ratio is by using a fraction.

Roberto's football team **lost 3** games and **won 7** games. What is the ratio of games lost to games won?

**Compare:**

games lost $\longrightarrow \dfrac{3}{7}$
games won $\longrightarrow$    The ratio is read **"3 to 7."**

**Write each ratio as a fraction.**

A. 5 cheetahs to 7 tigers _____

B. 12 trumpets to 5 violins _____

C. Jill's 23¢ to Bob's 45¢ _____

D. 1 meter to 4 meters _____

20 tulips to 13 roses _____

4 taxis to 9 buses _____

10 chairs to 3 tables _____

3 minutes to 25 minutes _____

**Use the information in the pictures to write each ratio as a fraction.**

E. soccer balls to footballs _____

F. baseballs to soccer balls _____

G. footballs to soccer balls _____

H. baseballs to all balls _____

**Use the information in the table to write each ratio as a fraction.**

I. Seattle: games won to games lost _____

J. Atlanta: games won to games played _____

K. Oakland: games lost to games played _____

L. Chicago: games lost to games won _____

| Team | Win | Loss |
|---------|-----|------|
| Seattle | 48 | 54 |
| Atlanta | 57 | 47 |
| Oakland | 62 | 42 |
| Chicago | 44 | 60 |

## EQUAL RATIOS

Camille reads **2 books** every **3 weeks**. At that rate, how many books will she read in **12 weeks**?

You need to find a ratio equal to $\frac{2}{3}$ with a denominator of 12.

**Compare:**

$\dfrac{\text{number of books} \longrightarrow}{\text{number of weeks} \longrightarrow} \dfrac{2}{3} = \dfrac{n}{12} \begin{matrix} \longleftarrow \text{books} \\ \longleftarrow \text{weeks} \end{matrix}$

$\dfrac{2}{3} = \dfrac{2 \times \mathbf{4}}{3 \times \mathbf{4}} = \dfrac{\mathbf{8}}{12}$  So, Camille will read **8 books** in 12 weeks.

**Solve for each variable.**

A.  $\dfrac{5}{6} = \dfrac{n}{36}$           $\dfrac{3}{8} = \dfrac{n}{24}$           $\dfrac{5}{7} = \dfrac{n}{42}$           $\dfrac{8}{9} = \dfrac{n}{63}$

  $n = $ _____        $n = $ _____        $n = $ _____        $n = $ _____

**Use equal ratios to solve each problem.**

B.  The Dollar-Mart grocery store sells 6 bars of soap for $1.00. How many bars of soap can a customer buy with $9.00?     $n = $ _____

C.  Kelsey's soccer team scored 5 points in 2 games. At this rate, how many points will the team score in 16 games?     $n = $ _____

D.  The O'Neil family drove 60 miles per hour. If they continue to drive at this speed, how many miles will they drive in 4 hours?     $n = $ _____

E.  Mia's mother works 40 hours each week. How many hours will Mia's mother work in 10 weeks?     $n = $ _____

F.  Zack bought 4 pounds of grapes for 16 people. How many pounds of grapes will he need for 48 people?     $n = $ _____

G.  The Wilson family's car gets 35 miles per gallon of gas. The car's gas tank holds 10 gallons. How many miles can the Wilsons drive on a tank of gas?     $n = $ _____

**114**

## SOLVING PROPORTIONS

An equation showing the equality of two ratios, such as $\frac{3}{7} = \frac{9}{21}$, is called a

**proportion**. The cross products in a proportion are always equal.

In a proportion, if $\frac{a}{b} = \frac{c}{d}$ then $a \times d = b \times c$.

 $3 \times 21 = 7 \times 9$

**Example:** Find the missing term in the proportion $\frac{2}{5} = \frac{n}{25}$

| Identify the terms to be multiplied. These are cross products. | Set the cross products equal to each other. | Solve. |
|---|---|---|
| | $2 \cdot 25 = 5 \cdot n$ | $5 \cdot n = 2 \cdot 25$ $5 \cdot n = 50$ $n = 50 \div 5$ $\boldsymbol{n = 10}$ |

**Use cross products to solve each proportion.**

A.   $\frac{5}{2} = \frac{10}{m}$          $\frac{3}{a} = \frac{9}{3}$          $\frac{12}{d} = \frac{3}{1}$          $\frac{7}{n} = \frac{2}{4}$

B.   $\frac{p}{15} = \frac{6}{5}$          $\frac{14}{21} = \frac{j}{3}$          $\frac{120}{30} = \frac{s}{5}$          $\frac{y}{18} = \frac{3}{6}$

C.   $\frac{100}{20} = \frac{5}{r}$          $\frac{24}{k} = \frac{8}{12}$          $\frac{g}{15} = \frac{8}{5}$          $\frac{5}{5} = \frac{7}{t}$

D.   $\frac{12}{5} = \frac{24}{b}$          $\frac{27}{18} = \frac{9}{m}$          $\frac{30}{25} = \frac{r}{10}$          $\frac{n}{21} = \frac{2}{14}$

# STANDARD MEASUREMENT

The charts show relationships between some standard measurements for length, weight, and capacity. To convert a smaller unit to a larger unit, divide. To convert a larger unit to a smaller unit, multiply.

| **Units of Length** |
| --- |
| 12 inches (in.) = 1 foot (ft.) |
| 3 feet = 1 yard (yd.) |
| 36 inches = 1 yard |
| 5,280 feet = 1 mile (mi.) |
| 1,760 yards = 1 mile |

| **Units of Weight** |
| --- |
| 16 ounces (oz.) = 1 pound (lb.) |
| 2,000 pounds = 1 ton (tn.) |

| **Units of Capacity** |
| --- |
| 8 fluid ounces (fl. oz.) = 1 cup (c.) |
| 2 cups = 1 pint (pt.) |
| 16 fluid ounces = 1 pint |
| 2 pints = 1 quart (qt.) |
| 4 quarts = 1 gallon (gal.) |

51 ft. = _____ yd.
**Think:** You are going from a smaller unit to a larger unit, so divide.
3 ft. = 1 yd.
51 ÷ 3 = 17
51 ft. = **17 yd.**

64 oz. = _____ lb.
**Think:** You are going from a smaller unit to a larger unit, so divide.
1 lb. = 16 oz.
64 ÷ 16 = 4
64 oz. = **4 lb.**

5 qt. = _____ pt.
**Think:** You are going from a larger unit to a smaller unit, so multiply.
1 qt. = 2 pt.
5 x 2 = 10
5 qt. = **10 pt.**

## Write each equivalent measure.

A.  2 mi. = _____ ft.          1 ft. 3 in. = _____ in.          4 yd. = _____ ft.

B.  60 in. = _____ ft.          5,280 yd. = _____ mi.          144 in. = _____ yd.

C.  1 qt. = _____ pt.          3 gal. = _____ qt.          1 pt. = _____ fl. oz.

D.  16 c. = _____ gal.          4 pt. = _____ qt.          22 pt. = _____ qt.

E.  96 oz. = _____ lb.          3 lb. = _____ oz.          7 tn. = _____ lb.

F.  9 lb. 3 oz. = _____ oz.          10,000 lb. = _____ tn.          32,000 oz. = _____ tn.

## Use >, <, or = to compare each pair of measurements.

G.  4 ft. 4 in. ☐ 56 in.          7,020 ft. ☐ 4 mi.          10 fl. oz. ☐ 1 c.

H.  5 qt. ☐ 2 gal.          320 oz. ☐ 10 lb.          3 lb. ☐ 50 oz.

# METRIC MEASUREMENT

The charts show the relationships between some metric measurements for length, weight, and capacity. To convert a smaller unit to a larger unit, divide. To convert a larger unit to a smaller unit, multiply.

**Units of Length**
10 millimeters (mm) = 1 centimeter (cm)
10 centimeters = 1 decimeter (dm)
10 decimeters = 1 meter (m)
10 meters = 1 dekameter (dam)
10 dekameters = 1 hectometer (hm)
10 hectometers = 1 kilometer (km)

**Units of Capacity**
10 milliliters (mL) = 1 centiliter (cL)
10 centiliters = 1 deciliter (dL)
10 deciliters = 1 liter (L)
10 liters = 1 dekaliter (daL)
10 dekaliters = 1 hectoliter (hL)
10 hectoliters = 1 kiloliter (kL)

**Units of Weight**
10 milligrams (mg) = 1 centigram (cg)
10 centigrams = 1 decigram (dg)
10 decigrams = 1 gram (g)
10 grams = 1 dekagram (dag)
10 dekagrams = 1 hectogram (hg)
10 hectograms = 1 kilogram (kg)

**Write each equivalent measure.**

A.  7 m = _____ cm          6 m = _____ dm          3,500 cm = _____ m

B.  82 dm = _____ cm        8 km = _____ m          19,000 m = _____ km

C.  3 g = _____ kg          45 dag = _____ g        66,000 mg = _____ g

D.  4 kg = _____ mg         708 mg = _____ dg       35 kg = _____ g

E.  9 daL = _____ L         6,800 mL = _____ L      25 dL = _____ mL

F.  2.5 kL = _____ daL      14,000 L = _____ kL     520 L = _____ mL

**Use >, <, or = to compare each pair of measurements.**

G.  25 mm ☐ 3 m          107 km ☐ 3,000 m          5,000 mg ☐ 5 kg

H.  28 g ☐ 700 mg        5 L ☐ 500 mL              600,000 mL ☐ 60 L

# MEASURING ANGLES

You can measure an angle using an instrument called a **protractor**.

Measure ∠ ABC.

Place the center of the protractor at **point B**, the **vertex** of the angle.

Align the zero mark on **BC**, one side of the angle.

Read the measure of the angle where **BA**, the other side of the angle, crosses the protractor.

The measure of ∠ **ABC** = **70°**.

You can classify angles by their measurement.

**right angle** ⟶ measures **exactly 90°**

**acute angle** ⟶ measures **less than 90°**

**obtuse angle** ⟶ measures **greater than 90°** but **less than 180°**

**Use a protractor to measure each angle. Then, write the measurement and classify the angle as acute, right, or obtuse.**

A.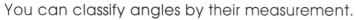

_____    _____    _____

B.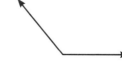

_____    _____    _____

C.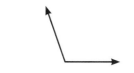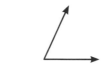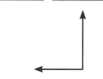

_____    _____    _____

D.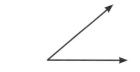

_____    _____    _____

# CLASSIFYING TRIANGLES BY THEIR ANGLES

A **triangle** is a closed figure made from three line segments. The **sum of the angles** in any triangle always equals **180°**. Triangles can be classified by the sizes of their angles.

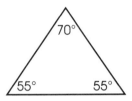

An **acute triangle** has three acute angles.

A **right triangle** has exactly one right angle.

An **obtuse triangle** has exactly one obtuse angle.

Find the measure of the missing angle in the triangle. Classify the triangle as *acute*, *right*, or *obtuse*. Remember, the sum of the angles will equal 180°.

a

| | |
|---|---|
| Write an equation using the given angles. | $a + 35 + 60 = 180$ |
| | $35 + 60 = 95$ |
| Add the given angles. | $a + 95 = 180$ |
| Solve the equation. | $a = 180 - 95$ |
| | $a = \mathbf{85°}$ |

All three angles of the triangle are less than 90°. The triangle is **acute**.

**Find the measure of the missing angle in each triangle. Then classify, the triangle as acute, right, or obtuse.**

A.

a = _____

_____

c = _____

_____

b = _____

_____

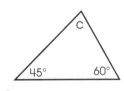

c = _____

_____

B.

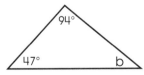

b = _____

_____

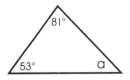

a = _____

_____

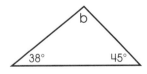

b = _____

_____

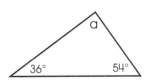

a = _____

_____

# AREAS OF TRIANGLES AND PARALLELOGRAMS

Find the area of the triangle.

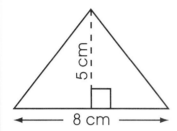

The area (A) of a triangle is equal to $\frac{1}{2}$ the base (b) times the height (h).

$$A = \frac{1}{2} \cdot b \cdot h$$

$$A = \frac{1}{2} \cdot 8 \cdot 5 = 20$$

The area of the triangle is **20 cm²**.

Find the area of the parallelogram.

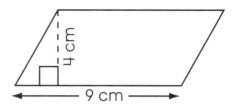

The area (A) of a parallelogram is equal to the base (b) times the height (h).

$$A = b \cdot h$$

$$A = 9 \cdot 4 = 36$$

The area of the parallelogram is **36 m²**.

## Find the area of each figure.

A.

A = _____ cm²

A = _____ in.²

A = _____ ft.²

B.

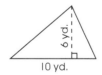

A = _____ yd.²

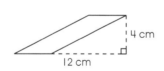

A = _____ cm²

A = _____ cm²

C.

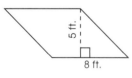

A = _____ ft.²

A = _____ in.²

A = _____ m²

# ANSWER KEY

## Page 4

A. 11; 16; 11; 7; 14; 14; B. 5; 8; 7; 8; 4; 8; C. 48; 28; 45; 56; 27; 16; D. 9; 8; 9; 8; 7; 3; E. 5,233; 934; 335; 49,378; 2,629; 1,455; F. 23,496; 3,726; 21,580; 177,261; 278,048; 2,473,515; G. 78; 329 r4; 381 r31; 264 r11; 5 r18; 82 r47

## Page 5

A. Answers will vary but may include: $\frac{4}{6}$, $\frac{6}{8}$, $\frac{4}{10}$, $\frac{10}{14}$, $\frac{2}{4}$, $\frac{14}{16}$; B. $\frac{7}{10}$, $\frac{1}{4}$, $\frac{1}{4}$, $\frac{2}{3}$, $\frac{5}{12}$, $\frac{1}{2}$; C. >, <, >, >; D. $8\frac{1}{6}$, $5\frac{1}{6}$, $\frac{16}{5}$, $\frac{69}{10}$, $4\frac{1}{3}$, $\frac{101}{8}$; E. 1, $\frac{2}{5}$, $\frac{1}{3}$; F. $\frac{1}{3}$, $\frac{2}{3}$, $1\frac{1}{3}$; G. $7\frac{3}{5}$, $7\frac{3}{5}$, $4\frac{1}{2}$, $3\frac{1}{2}$

## Page 6

A. $1\frac{4}{9}$, $4\frac{4}{5}$, $1\frac{1}{2}$, $7\frac{7}{12}$, $16\frac{2}{9}$; B. $\frac{11}{12}$, $\frac{5}{16}$, $\frac{1}{5}$, $\frac{5}{21}$, $\frac{11}{20}$; C. $\frac{15}{28}$, $29\frac{7}{10}$, $1\frac{1}{15}$, $3\frac{3}{7}$; D. $1\frac{17}{18}$, $6\frac{1}{4}$, $1\frac{5}{9}$, $3\frac{19}{27}$; E. 16 students

## Page 7

A. 10.45, 33.00, 106.042, 16.598, 361.208; B. 2.49, 36.6, 22.06, 64.746, 4.2; C. 2.4, 45.64, 1.38, 154.66, 12.9948; D. 0.98, 1.3, 2.4, 3.9; E. 0.000515, 0.003552, 0.65, 0.009; F. 0.7, 0.92, 3.2, 4.16, 0.625; G. 25%, 72%, 54%, 99%, 8%; H. $62.40

## Page 8

A. 11, 6, 12; add 6, subtract 5; 66, 67, 201; multiply by 3, add 1; B. 11, 12, 13, 14; x + 7 = y; 5, 6, 7, 8; x ÷ 2 = y; C. c = 6; g = 56; d = 10; b = 49; D. n = 56; p = 8; y = 3; k = 42; E. mean: 39.2, mode: 25, median: 39, range: 37; mean: 5.5, mode: 6, median: 5.5, range: 6; F. 36; 2; 64; G. 5; 6,000; 7; H. right, 10 in.²; acute, 24 cm²

## Page 10

A. 7, 14, 11, 3, 10, 15, 6; B. 17, 8, 12, 4, 10, 5, 8; C. 18, 11, 10, 15, 12, 16, 6; D. 12, 8, 14, 12, 16, 9, 17; E. 9, 9, 4, 15, 14, 13, 14; F. 13, 9, 13, 11, 11, 5, 6; G. 6, 16, 13, 12, 16, 11, 4; H. 10, 7, 10, 11, 12, 11, 10

## Page 11

A. 71; 801; 1,164; 553; 1,446; 550; B. 794; 982; 1,262; 1,516; 535; 8,967; C. 2,119; 4,643; 4,339; 16,519; 5,691; 13,903; D. 11,601; 10,062; 10,756; 82,780; 96,057; 53,229; E. 117,142; 59,429; 33,171; 74,171; 71,391; 107,121

## Page 12

A. 143; 108; 978; 664; 1,073; 958; B. 576; 838; 992; 1,133; 1,779; 1,270; C. 4,808; 5,741; 6,891; 10,608; 4,976; 8,624; D. 7,556; 10,244; 115,246; 87,254; 17,514; 23,273

## Page 13

A. 9, 3, 9, 7, 9, 4, 8; B. 9, 8, 7, 8, 4, 5, 3; C. 4, 4, 7, 6, 6, 6, 2; D. 7, 7, 7, 8, 9, 6, 9; E. 10, 7, 5, 6, 1, 5, 6; F. 2, 3, 5, 3, 5, 1, 3; G. 5, 8, 3, 5, 6, 8, 8; H. 9, 6, 4, 2, 9, 2, 4

## Page 14

A. 118; 199; 314; 65; 614; 349; B. 384; 81; 188; 387; 397; 132; C. 129; 148; 246; 60; 429; 93; D. 8,530; 4,629; 7,801; 1,289; 1,491; 3,095; E. 695; 2,893; 588; 20,356; 43,479; 428,613

## Page 15

A. 176; 2,032; 164; 2,709; 3,551; 1,624; B. 5,283; 1,749; 5,001; 3,580; 3,923; 4,406; C. 77,841; 56,154; 32,418; 87,568; 74,168; 28,452; D. 24,028; 59,579; 345,439; 201,057; 631,842; 475,948; E. 372,236; 771,172; 90,001; 192,853; 671,718; 533,334

## Page 16

A. 34,696 people; B. 1,300,611 people; C. 344,657 people; D. 63 feet; E. 224 feet; F. 2,986 feet

# ANSWER KEY

**Page 17**

A. 383 books; B. 5,692 books; C. 6,750 books;
D. 8,250 books; E. 21 books; F. 83

**Page 18**

A. 850; 485; 454; 5,009; 9,741; B. 423; 5,971; 814;
1,791; 3,712; C. 4,806; 25,245; 28,512; 112,294; 83,174;
D. 1,366; 1,709; 6,552; 1,628; 1,623; E. 78,702; 31,577;
21,757; 193,744; 715,413; F. 10,533 people; 85,711
people; G. 1,781 vehicles

**Page 19**

A. 242; 733; 7,586; 8,925; 9,011; B. 455; 853; 588;
6,309; 1,154; C. 15,464; 37,707; 163,864; 108,718;
177,974; D. 5,458; 35,788; 23,528; 33,890;
375,649; E. 5,059; 10,322; 27,983; 1,900; 6,989;
F. 15,473 games; 115,947 games; G. 7,585 visits

**Page 20**

A. 24, 3, 63, 24, 49, 40, 42; B. 6, 54, 20, 36, 36, 72,
45; C. 64, 10, 4, 24, 45, 21, 48; D. 28, 35, 4, 5, 28, 72,
18; E. 56, 12, 25, 8, 54, 32, 15; F. 81, 6, 63, 30, 14, 7,
36; G. 30, 32, 35, 16, 9, 12, 8; H. 9, 48, 27, 56, 16,
40, 18

**Page 21**

A. 425; 360; 116; 147; 434; B. 4,581; 844; 1,680; 5,598;
2,505; C. 2,896; 4,205; 1,611; 4,314; 5,679; D. 22,050;
52,290; 24,305; 27,849; 60,298; E. 137,620; 256,236;
237,402; 193,672; 605,032

**Page 22**

A. 1,850; 1,888; 2,304; 3,416; 1,092; B. 2,112; 4,902;
5,952; 2,808; 3,230; C. 23,825; 16,872; 16,568; 39,704;
16,974; D. 76,342; 61,866; 34,992; 61,855; 40,768;
E. 205,179; 289,902; 157,534; 617,768; 391,902

**Page 23**

A. 290,322; 372,723; 572,286; 856,304; 260,766;
B. 82,369; 332,762; 136,125; 236,572; 171,720;
C. 1,101,790; 1,210,808; 480,075; 385,985; 547,328;

**Page 24**

A. 9, 5, 9, 8, 6, 8, 2; B. 6, 8, 1, 4, 7, 3, 6; C. 3, 5, 7, 5,
2, 9, 5; D. 7, 8, 6, 4, 5, 4, 4; E. 4, 3, 2, 9, 7, 9, 6;
F. 8, 6, 7, 4, 8, 3, 9; G. 2, 1, 9, 3, 6, 8, 5; H. 4, 2, 8, 7,
1, 5, 6

**Page 25**

A. 18, 38, 216, 51, 16; B. 214 r1; 214 r1; 112 r2; 113 r4;
201 r2; C. 211 r4; 270 r4; 913 r1; 512 r2; 708 r2

**Page 26**

A. 18 r29; 22 r19; 260 r9; 31 r23; B. 222 r8; 252 r3;
42 r3; 122 r61; C. 96 r7; 50 r47; 2,333 r1; 2,025 r43

**Page 27**

A. 6, 8, 7; 4 r408; B. 70 r101; 7 r6; 34 r72; 273 r89;
C. 309 r10; 501 r18; 274 r160; 400 r78

**Page 28**

A. 128 people; B. 10 times; C. 40 minutes;
D. 8 minutes; E. 135 times; F. 1,536 people

**Page 29**

A. 1,300 quarts; B. 9 years; C. 6 gallons;
D. 180 small bags; E. 14 trucks; F. 3 boxes

**Page 30**

A. 553; 1,705; 294; 14,573; 12,594; B. 35,376; 154,361;
36,014; 705,200; 4,688,688; C. 9; 16; 91; 1,419;
D. 68 r47; 210 r24; 57 r51; 406 r52; E. 3,276 miles;
F. 9 blankets, 8 feet

**Page 31**

A. 148; 2,490; 43,902; 9,394; B. 33,628; 91,874;
221,714; 111,606; C. 9; 92; 9 r3; 120 r5; D. 903 r2; 3 r9;
30 r10; 86 r96; E. $93,080; G. 110 marbles; 7 marbles

**Page 32**

A. $\frac{1}{8}$, $\frac{1}{4}$, $\frac{4}{8}$, $\frac{7}{8}$; B. $\frac{1}{10}$, $\frac{2}{5}$, $\frac{5}{10}$, $\frac{3}{5}$, $\frac{9}{10}$;
C. $\frac{2}{12}$, $\frac{4}{12}$, $\frac{2}{3}$, $\frac{9}{12}$, $\frac{12}{12}$

# ANSWER KEY

**Page 33**

A.–D. Answers will vary.; E. $\frac{3}{33}$, $\frac{5}{20}$, $\frac{8}{32}$, $\frac{48}{54}$ ;

F. $\frac{9}{45}$, $\frac{12}{36}$, $\frac{15}{48}$, $\frac{9}{24}$; G. $\frac{6}{36}$, $\frac{36}{54}$, $\frac{3}{90}$, $\frac{6}{33}$ ;

G. $\frac{42}{66}$, $\frac{20}{50}$, $\frac{30}{120}$, $\frac{35}{49}$

**Page 34**

A. GCF: 6; B. GCF: 5; C. GCF: 8; D. GCF: 7;
E. GCF: 7; F. GCF: 3; G. GCF: 9; H. GCF: 4;
I. GCF: 5; J. GCF: 3; K. GCF: 7; L. GCF: 5

**Page 35**

A. $\frac{2}{3}$, $\frac{1}{2}$, $\frac{3}{5}$, $\frac{4}{7}$, $\frac{1}{5}$; B. $\frac{1}{9}$, $\frac{1}{3}$, $\frac{5}{6}$, $\frac{14}{15}$,

$\frac{1}{4}$; C. $\frac{2}{7}$, $\frac{2}{3}$, $\frac{11}{15}$, $\frac{1}{2}$, $\frac{7}{10}$; D. $\frac{1}{3}$, $\frac{1}{2}$, $\frac{4}{5}$,

$\frac{1}{2}$, $\frac{11}{16}$; E. $\frac{1}{2}$, $\frac{1}{4}$, $\frac{13}{14}$, $\frac{1}{5}$, $\frac{15}{16}$

**Page 36**

A. LCM: 6; B. LCM: 8; C. LCM: 15; D. LCM: 12;
E. LCM: 24; F. LCM: 30; G. LCM: 30; H. LCM: 36;
I. LCM: 40; J. LCM:30

**Page 37**

A. $\frac{1}{9}$, $\frac{3}{9}$, $\frac{2}{6}$, $\frac{1}{6}$, $\frac{25}{30}$, $\frac{12}{30}$; B. $\frac{9}{24}$, $\frac{16}{24}$, $\frac{3}{9}$, $\frac{4}{9}$,

$\frac{36}{45}$, $\frac{25}{45}$; C. $\frac{14}{28}$, $\frac{12}{28}$, $\frac{16}{24}$, $\frac{21}{24}$, $\frac{18}{30}$, $\frac{25}{30}$; D. $\frac{2}{16}$, $\frac{1}{16}$,

$\frac{1}{12}$, $\frac{3}{12}$, $\frac{1}{18}$, $\frac{2}{18}$; E. $\frac{9}{36}$, $\frac{10}{36}$, $\frac{24}{56}$, $\frac{21}{56}$, $\frac{11}{22}$, $\frac{8}{22}$

**Page 38**

A. =, >, >, <; B. >, <, >, >; C. $\frac{1}{3} < \frac{7}{12} < \frac{5}{6}$ ;

$\frac{3}{4} < \frac{13}{16} < \frac{7}{8}$ ; $\frac{9}{14} < \frac{5}{7} < \frac{3}{4}$ ; D. $\frac{1}{2} < \frac{3}{4} < \frac{5}{6}$ ;

$\frac{3}{8} < \frac{3}{5} < \frac{3}{4}$ ; $\frac{3}{4} < \frac{4}{5} < \frac{17}{20}$

**Page 39**

A. $\frac{4}{5}$ of the pizza; B. $\frac{3}{8}$ of the pizza; C. 32 pizzas;

D. a. green peppers; b. mushrooms

**Page 40**

A. Shopping and Outdoor Recreation;

B. $\frac{3}{16}$ of the tourists; C. $\frac{3}{4}$ of the tourists;

D. Outdoor Recreation; E. $\frac{1}{4}$ of the tourists;

F. Museums; G. Theme Parks

**Page 41**

A. $\frac{2}{5}$, $\frac{3}{5}$, $\frac{5}{5}$; B. $\frac{12}{16}$, $\frac{3}{4}$, $\frac{21}{28}$, $\frac{30}{40}$; C. 11, 7, 12, 10;

D. $\frac{2}{3}$, $\frac{3}{10}$, $\frac{2}{9}$; E. 20, 36, 36, 15; F. 8, 15, 24, 30;

G. >, >, >

**Page 42**

A. $\frac{2}{8}$, $\frac{2}{4}$, $\frac{5}{8}$, $\frac{6}{8}$; B. $\frac{3}{8}$, $\frac{9}{24}$, $\frac{12}{32}$; C. 5, 5, 6, 20;

D. $\frac{3}{4}$, $\frac{7}{8}$, $\frac{1}{3}$; E. 60, 60, 28, 35; F. 9, 20, 20;

G. >, <, >

**Page 43**

A. $1\frac{1}{3}$, $2\frac{1}{2}$, 5, $1\frac{5}{12}$, $8\frac{2}{3}$; B. $3\frac{1}{3}$, 9, $3\frac{4}{13}$,

$6\frac{1}{5}$, $6\frac{2}{3}$

**Page 44**

A. $\frac{26}{3}$, $\frac{27}{5}$, $\frac{5}{2}$, $\frac{35}{8}$; B. $\frac{27}{4}$, $\frac{114}{37}$, $\frac{32}{3}$, $\frac{51}{4}$; C. $\frac{52}{5}$,

$\frac{122}{11}$, $\frac{23}{16}$, $\frac{26}{3}$; D. $\frac{41}{6}$, $\frac{29}{8}$, $\frac{81}{16}$, $\frac{151}{12}$; E. $\frac{5}{5}$, $\frac{12}{12}$,

$\frac{8}{2}$, $\frac{24}{4}$; F. $\frac{24}{3}$, $\frac{30}{3}$, $\frac{60}{5}$, $\frac{32}{2}$; G. $\frac{54}{3}$, $\frac{55}{5}$, $\frac{26}{2}$, $\frac{75}{5}$

**Page 45**

A. $\frac{1}{7}$, 1, $\frac{1}{2}$; B. $1\frac{2}{3}$, $\frac{2}{3}$, $1\frac{1}{5}$; C. $\frac{7}{20}$, $\frac{6}{11}$, $\frac{1}{2}$;

D. $1\frac{1}{3}$, $1\frac{2}{5}$, 1; E. $\frac{3}{5}$, $1\frac{3}{7}$, $\frac{1}{4}$; F. $\frac{3}{8}$, $\frac{5}{12}$, $\frac{2}{9}$

**Page 46**

A. 5, $4\frac{2}{5}$, $4\frac{2}{3}$, 6, $1\frac{1}{3}$; B. 9, $1\frac{2}{3}$, 2, $1\frac{1}{2}$, $10\frac{2}{5}$;

C. $2\frac{3}{5}$, $7\frac{1}{2}$, $3\frac{4}{7}$, $15\frac{4}{15}$, $9\frac{3}{5}$

**Page 47**

A. $4\frac{8}{9}$, $1\frac{3}{4}$, $2\frac{1}{3}$, $3\frac{1}{2}$, $5\frac{4}{5}$; B. $2\frac{5}{7}$, $1\frac{4}{5}$, $4\frac{3}{5}$, $5\frac{3}{4}$, $6\frac{7}{8}$; C. $5\frac{3}{4}$, $4\frac{1}{2}$, $2\frac{1}{4}$, $11\frac{7}{9}$, $13\frac{5}{9}$

**Page 48**

A. $4\frac{2}{5}$, $4\frac{7}{8}$, $5\frac{4}{9}$; B. $2\frac{4}{5}$, $\frac{1}{2}$, $2\frac{3}{4}$; C. $3\frac{3}{4}$, $3\frac{2}{3}$, $9\frac{2}{3}$; D. $5\frac{4}{5}$, $6\frac{7}{8}$, $9\frac{3}{5}$

**Page 49**

A. $\frac{11}{12}$, $\frac{7}{18}$, $1\frac{1}{10}$, $\frac{1}{8}$, $\frac{2}{9}$; B. $1\frac{5}{24}$, $1\frac{3}{8}$, $\frac{1}{15}$, $1\frac{1}{20}$, $\frac{29}{42}$; C. $\frac{1}{5}$, $1\frac{3}{10}$, $\frac{2}{15}$, $1\frac{2}{9}$, $\frac{37}{40}$; D. $\frac{1}{12}$, $\frac{3}{10}$, $\frac{1}{6}$, $1\frac{5}{21}$, $\frac{16}{35}$

**Page 50**

A. $8\frac{1}{6}$, $13\frac{5}{12}$, $9\frac{5}{8}$, $17\frac{3}{20}$, $3\frac{11}{12}$; B. $19\frac{5}{24}$, $61\frac{4}{5}$, $24\frac{8}{9}$, $8\frac{7}{9}$, $13\frac{11}{12}$; C. $13\frac{13}{24}$, $14\frac{17}{24}$, $6\frac{5}{6}$, $28\frac{3}{8}$, $14\frac{1}{2}$

**Page 51**

A. $1\frac{13}{16}$, $3\frac{5}{7}$, $5\frac{11}{15}$, $3\frac{1}{2}$; B. $3\frac{5}{9}$, $1\frac{3}{10}$, $\frac{5}{16}$, $3\frac{13}{20}$; C. $8\frac{1}{6}$, $12\frac{7}{8}$, $12\frac{11}{15}$, $3\frac{25}{42}$

**Page 52**

A. $1\frac{1}{4}$ cups of raisins; B. 4 cups of peanuts; C. $\frac{3}{8}$ cup more candy-coated chocolate pieces; D. $4\frac{1}{8}$ cups of trail mix

**Page 53**

A. $2\frac{1}{2}$ games; B. $\frac{5}{8}$ inches wider; C. $\frac{7}{24}$ of the fans; D. $\frac{19}{24}$ of his money

**Page 54**

A. $\frac{7}{3}$, $\frac{35}{8}$, $\frac{33}{5}$, $\frac{71}{6}$; B. $3\frac{2}{7}$, $6\frac{1}{2}$, $7\frac{1}{2}$, $5\frac{5}{16}$; C. $\frac{4}{5}$, $1\frac{1}{4}$, $1\frac{1}{15}$, $\frac{13}{18}$; D. $\frac{2}{3}$, $\frac{7}{12}$, $\frac{7}{60}$, $\frac{1}{3}$; E. 11, $5\frac{1}{10}$, $4\frac{5}{12}$, $5\frac{5}{42}$; F. $4\frac{1}{4}$ hours; G. $2\frac{3}{16}$ inches

**Page 55**

A. $\frac{7}{5}$, $\frac{23}{4}$, $\frac{23}{6}$, $\frac{103}{8}$; B. $5\frac{3}{5}$, $6\frac{1}{3}$, $3\frac{1}{3}$, $4\frac{4}{5}$; C. $\frac{5}{7}$, $1\frac{1}{3}$, $1\frac{3}{20}$, $1\frac{1}{25}$; D. $\frac{3}{7}$, $\frac{5}{12}$, $\frac{3}{20}$, $\frac{17}{45}$; E. 9, $9\frac{3}{10}$, $4\frac{35}{72}$, $8\frac{7}{9}$; F. $\frac{7}{15}$ of her video collection; G. $1\frac{5}{8}$ inches

**Page 56**

A. $\frac{1}{40}$, $\frac{1}{28}$, $\frac{1}{96}$; B. $\frac{12}{35}$, $\frac{3}{5}$, $\frac{8}{21}$; C. $\frac{2}{3}$, $\frac{7}{12}$, $\frac{56}{81}$; D. $\frac{1}{12}$, $\frac{2}{9}$, $\frac{3}{16}$; E. $\frac{21}{50}$, $\frac{10}{49}$, $\frac{4}{9}$; F. $\frac{9}{28}$, $\frac{5}{12}$, $\frac{5}{12}$

**Page 57**

A. $\frac{1}{3}$, $2\frac{1}{2}$, $\frac{1}{2}$; B. $1\frac{3}{5}$, $2\frac{1}{2}$, $1\frac{1}{2}$; C. $2\frac{1}{4}$, $1\frac{1}{3}$, $3\frac{1}{3}$; D. $1\frac{4}{5}$, 1, $1\frac{1}{2}$; E. $\frac{4}{5}$, $4\frac{1}{6}$, $2\frac{1}{2}$; F. $1\frac{4}{11}$, $1\frac{1}{6}$, $1\frac{11}{13}$

**Page 58**

A. $1\frac{1}{12}$, $1\frac{1}{10}$, $1\frac{1}{12}$; B. $2\frac{3}{8}$, $2\frac{5}{6}$, $\frac{19}{24}$; C. $1\frac{13}{20}$, $3\frac{3}{10}$, $\frac{9}{14}$; D. $\frac{21}{40}$, $\frac{9}{10}$, $1\frac{2}{5}$; E. $\frac{5}{8}$, $\frac{1}{4}$, $\frac{1}{2}$; F. $\frac{27}{44}$, $1\frac{1}{3}$, $\frac{13}{30}$

**Page 59**

A. $14\frac{1}{6}$, $2\frac{17}{30}$, $5\frac{5}{8}$; B. $2\frac{1}{2}$, $4\frac{41}{64}$, $13\frac{1}{8}$; C. $4\frac{1}{4}$, $4\frac{1}{12}$, $8\frac{13}{15}$; D. $4\frac{7}{8}$, $5\frac{13}{28}$, $3\frac{3}{35}$; E. $9\frac{1}{10}$, $1\frac{43}{45}$, $2\frac{25}{64}$; F. $3\frac{3}{7}$, $4\frac{1}{5}$, $1\frac{4}{9}$

# ANSWER KEY

## Page 60

A. 14, $15\frac{2}{5}$, $6\frac{3}{5}$; B. $2\frac{3}{4}$, $22\frac{1}{2}$, $16\frac{4}{5}$; C. 7, $5\frac{5}{8}$,

$7\frac{1}{2}$; D. $6\frac{6}{7}$, $8\frac{2}{5}$, 11; E. $6\frac{2}{3}$, $3\frac{1}{4}$, $14\frac{2}{5}$;

F. $25\frac{3}{5}$, $4\frac{1}{2}$, 8

## Page 61

A. 4, 20, 48, 33; B. 56, 30, 60, 84; C. $7\frac{1}{2}$, $21\frac{1}{3}$,

$58\frac{1}{2}$, $9\frac{1}{4}$; D. $12\frac{1}{2}$, $7\frac{1}{3}$, $8\frac{1}{3}$, $31\frac{1}{2}$; E. 16 girls;

F. 72 chocolate chip cookies

## Page 62

A. $\frac{1}{3}$; B. $2\frac{2}{3}$ cups; C. 2 cups; D. 401°F

## Page 63

A. $\frac{4}{9}$ of the original height; B. 8 minutes;
C. 144 birds

## Page 64

A. $\frac{1}{16}$, $\frac{1}{40}$, $\frac{8}{21}$, $\frac{9}{16}$; B. $\frac{3}{5}$, $\frac{12}{35}$, 6, $4\frac{2}{3}$; C. $2\frac{1}{2}$,

2, $1\frac{19}{20}$, $2\frac{2}{9}$; D. $\frac{8}{9}$, $\frac{5}{8}$, $7\frac{1}{5}$, $1\frac{5}{9}$; E. $4\frac{1}{3}$, $9\frac{3}{4}$,

14, $6\frac{2}{3}$; F. $10\frac{5}{8}$ miles; G. 14 newspapers

## Page 65

A. $\frac{2}{15}$, $\frac{4}{21}$, $\frac{5}{21}$, $\frac{5}{14}$; B. $\frac{2}{3}$, $\frac{1}{2}$, $\frac{8}{13}$, $\frac{8}{11}$; C. $\frac{9}{16}$,

$3\frac{1}{3}$, $1\frac{11}{24}$, $3\frac{43}{64}$; D. $1\frac{1}{9}$, $\frac{3}{10}$, $1\frac{1}{3}$, $3\frac{5}{9}$; E. $13\frac{1}{8}$,

$8\frac{8}{11}$, $12\frac{3}{8}$, $3\frac{103}{143}$; F. $6\frac{3}{8}$ yards; G. $13\frac{1}{2}$ yards

## Page 66

A. $\frac{5}{11}$, $\frac{4}{9}$, $\frac{1}{9}$, $\frac{10}{3}$; B. $\frac{7}{1}$, $\frac{8}{37}$, $\frac{11}{15}$, $\frac{6}{1}$; C. $\frac{4}{3}$,

$\frac{1}{3}$, $\frac{4}{9}$, $\frac{8}{61}$; D. $\frac{3}{17}$, $\frac{9}{7}$, $\frac{1}{27}$, $\frac{5}{11}$; E. $\frac{3}{1}$, $\frac{1}{22}$,

$\frac{7}{10}$, $\frac{8}{17}$

## Page 67

A. 7, 2, 2, $1\frac{11}{24}$; B. $13\frac{1}{2}$, $6\frac{2}{3}$, $8\frac{3}{4}$, $1\frac{5}{9}$; C. 1,

$\frac{1}{2}$, $\frac{3}{10}$, $\frac{3}{5}$; D. 5, 2, $\frac{5}{6}$, $\frac{3}{5}$

## Page 68

A. $13\frac{1}{2}$, 35, $\frac{1}{14}$; B. $6\frac{2}{3}$, $\frac{1}{8}$, $\frac{9}{40}$; C. $\frac{3}{8}$, $2\frac{2}{5}$,

$\frac{4}{15}$; D. $\frac{5}{18}$, $\frac{7}{12}$, 12

## Page 69

A. 4, $1\frac{3}{4}$, $1\frac{9}{25}$; B. $\frac{3}{4}$, 2, $3\frac{1}{6}$; C. $6\frac{2}{3}$, $4\frac{1}{2}$, $1\frac{1}{5}$;

D. $3\frac{3}{7}$, 3, $\frac{1}{2}$; E. $2\frac{1}{14}$, 3, $\frac{5}{6}$

## Page 70

A. 8 servings; B. $6\frac{1}{2}$ ounces; C. $1\frac{3}{4}$ pounds;

D. $\frac{3}{20}$ pound; E. $2\frac{1}{3}$ ounces; F. $\frac{11}{36}$ pound

## Page 71

A. $137\frac{1}{2}$ pounds; B. $75\frac{3}{5}$ pounds; C. 264 pounds;

D. 75 pounds

## Page 72

A. $\frac{3}{2}$, $\frac{4}{7}$, $\frac{2}{9}$, $\frac{1}{5}$, $\frac{3}{34}$; B. 24, 24, 30; C. 7, $6\frac{2}{3}$,

$\frac{15}{16}$; D. $\frac{10}{21}$, $5\frac{1}{3}$, $2\frac{3}{4}$; E. $\frac{1}{8}$, $\frac{3}{16}$, $\frac{9}{20}$; F. $1\frac{5}{8}$,

$1\frac{2}{3}$, $4\frac{4}{5}$; G. 5 beads; H. 4 days

## Page 73

A. $\frac{4}{3}$, $\frac{5}{8}$, $\frac{3}{16}$, $\frac{1}{7}$, $\frac{5}{51}$; B. 8, 20, 6, 6; C. $\frac{1}{2}$,

$\frac{5}{6}$, $1\frac{1}{4}$, $13\frac{1}{2}$; D. $3\frac{3}{5}$, $\frac{3}{16}$, $\frac{17}{48}$, $1\frac{4}{5}$; E. $\frac{4}{5}$,

$1\frac{1}{11}$, $1\frac{12}{19}$, $\frac{2}{3}$; F. 6 relay runners; G. $\frac{11}{12}$ of a foot

of licorice

# ANSWER KEY

**Page 74**

A. 9.68, 11.64, 60.70, 187.9, 88.267; B. 4.41, 27.99, 13.35, 11.19, 7.29; C. 8.718, 206.90, 65.65, 7.65, 2.396; D. 155.13, 67.333, 59.88; E. 1.16, 11.37, 4.989

**Page 75**

A. 1.37, 13.48, 12.013, 54.543, 122.218; B. 914.064, 171.369, 153.703, 70.027, 48.07; C. 1.29, 707.414, 495.723, 282.793, 525.425; D. 171.473, 105.003, 25.127; E. 83.118, 245.554, 834.243

**Page 76**

A. 5.44, 3.26, 2.3, 4.15, 3.24; B. 1.54, 18.77, 369.76, 99.06, 63.001; C. 19.427, 46.701, 2.23, 29.528, 14.21; D. 11.25, 3.152, 213.196; E. 6.05, 10.01, 265.441

**Page 77**

A. $23.74; B. $40.79; C. $74.71; D. $75.00; E. $13.65; F. $48.75

**Page 78**

A. 6.81 minutes, yes; B. 11.54 seconds; C. 11.77 seconds; D. 36.8 points, 1.1 points; E. 3.1 meters; F. add 0.125 meters, 3.7 meters

**Page 79**

A. 0.18, 8.484, 69.726; B. 0.23, 6.111, 15.161; C. 1.18, 16.183, 30.408; D. 0.026, 1.861, 15.773; E. $81.23; F. 37.3 seconds

**Page 80**

A. 0.79, 9.677, 28.347; B. 0.41, 6.032, 11.165; C. 1.34, 11.564, 51.438; D. 0.051, 1.942, 8.715; E. $46.27; F. 59.93 seconds

**Page 81**

A. 1,596.8; 159.68; 15.968; 159.68; 1.5968; B. 1,802.4; 180.24; 18.024; 180.24; 1.8024; C. 1,251.0; 125.10; 12.510; 125.10; 1.2510; D. 91.14; 138.82; 172.02; 21.142; 9.971; E. 65.1472; 40.6224; 31.2806; 86.8042; 3.6834

**Page 82**

A. 2.4, 2.7, 0.84, 39.2; B. 13.5, 11.24, 8.8, 18.18; C. 95.2, 80.6, 240.5, 2.38; D. 13.52, 4.368, 25,115.8, 291.928

**Page 83**

A. 0.28, 0.15, 0.324, 15.66; B. 5.04, 0.084, 0.18, 0.0264; C. 117.81, 0.405, 0.4344, 0.4002; D. 1.485, 1.56, 39.216, 22.4536

**Page 84**

A. 0.00182, 0.000504, 0.00387, 0.001; B. 0.001749, 0.000672, 0.00244, 0.00315; C. 0.0132, 0.0194, 0.015, 0.02451; D. 0.007912, 0.002875, 0.003901, 0.02781

**Page 85**

A. 22.5 miles; B. $4.10; C. $5.60; D. 42.55 hours; E. $2.31; F. 43.8 meters

**Page 86**

A. 63.65 mL; B. 56.096 mL; C. 136.8 cm; D. 0.63 kg; E. 116.56 calories; F. 2.1 cm

**Page 87**

A. 2.07, 0.48, 0.1685, 0.5328; B. 0.024, 0.009, 0.149, 0.02202; C. 0.222, 2.058, 37.74, 0.00729; D. 0.066, 0.204, 0.05166, 0.91735; E. 83.2 ounces; F. $2.16

**Page 88**

A. 1.26, 0.42, 0.1032, 2.7004; B. 0.063, 0.03, 0.1435, 0.02778; C. 0.243, 1.778, 76.36, 0.00186; D. 0.44415, 0.105, 0.0539, 0.09052; E. 67 ounces; F. 0.036 miles

**Page 89**

A. 0.3, 0.03, 0.23, 0.023; B. 22.7, 2.27, 4.91, 0.021; C. 20.1, 2.01, 0.61, 0.46; D. 0.98, 1.84, 0.949, 1.30

**Page 90**

A. 0.54, 1.15, 0.95, 1.825, 0.3125; B. 1.62, 1.575, 1.05, 0.838, 0.748; C. 13.35, 0.535, 1.34, 0.325, 0.175

**MATH SUCCESS** RB-904108

# ANSWER KEY

## Page 91

A. 0.08, 0.009, 0.07, 0.016, 0.065; B. 0.02375, 0.0902, 0.01775, 0.095, 0.00625; C. 0.03, 0.006, 0.013, 0.035, 0.033

## Page 92

A. 9, 0.2, 9.9, 0.8; B. 6.2, 7, 0.5, 0.8; C. 3, 4.3, 0.7, 0.3; D. 2.14, 0.97, 0.84, 0.17

## Page 93

A. $0.66/pound; B. $0.42 each; C. $0.22/ounce; D. $0.04/cup; E. $0.19/pound; F. $1.29

## Page 94

A. 200 trombones; B. 0.055 watts; C. 28 pianos; D. 0.08 watts

## Page 95

A. 0.9, 0.42, 0.23, 2.14; B. 8.03, 5.07, 0.009, 0.0063; C. 0.08, 2.3, 230, 36; D. 17, 20.9, 31,200, 156; E. $0.27/ounce; F. 10.6 feet

## Page 96

A. 0.6, 0.37, 0.12, 1.37; B. 5.09, 2.03, 0.003, 0.0037; C. 0.04, 1.5, 180, 25; D. 5, 435, 30, 320; E. $0.49/card; F. 7.82 grams

## Page 97

A. 0.8, 0.375, 0.6, 0.6, 0.76; B. 0.85, 0.04, 0.225, 0.72, 0.1875; C. 0.555, 0.3125, 0.225, 0.32, 0.475; D. 0.75, 0.6875, 0.5, 0.435, 0.12

## Page 98

A. $\frac{1}{10}$, $2\frac{3}{5}$, $\frac{2}{5}$, $6\frac{1}{2}$; B. $8\frac{7}{10}$, $\frac{9}{10}$, $4\frac{4}{5}$, $\frac{3}{10}$;
C. $\frac{1}{5}$, $\frac{1}{4}$, $\frac{11}{20}$, $6\frac{17}{50}$; D. $8\frac{2}{25}$, $\frac{1}{25}$, $\frac{1}{100}$, $4\frac{3}{50}$;
E. $\frac{21}{50}$, $1\frac{3}{4}$, $\frac{61}{125}$, $\frac{43}{50}$; F. $2\frac{1}{2}$, $\frac{101}{200}$, $3\frac{101}{250}$, $\frac{133}{250}$;
G. $7\frac{133}{250}$, $\frac{11}{40}$, $9\frac{227}{250}$, $\frac{211}{250}$

## Page 99

A. 9%, 4%, 30%, 50%; B. 80%, 10%, 100%, 14 %;

Equivalent Ratio: $\frac{50}{100}$, $\frac{33}{100}$, $\frac{65}{100}$, $\frac{56}{100}$, $\frac{30}{100}$, $\frac{5}{100}$,

$\frac{98}{100}$, $\frac{7}{100}$; Fraction in Lowest Terms: $\frac{1}{2}$, $\frac{33}{100}$, $\frac{13}{20}$,

$\frac{14}{25}$, $\frac{3}{10}$, $\frac{1}{20}$, $\frac{49}{50}$, $\frac{7}{100}$

## Page 100

A. 75%, 25%, 50%, 10%; B. 11%, 73%, 20%, 5%;

C. 60%, 90%, 13%, 89%; D. $\frac{1}{25}$, $\frac{4}{25}$, $\frac{1}{4}$, $\frac{17}{50}$;

E. $\frac{3}{4}$, $\frac{3}{20}$, $\frac{1}{5}$, $\frac{13}{100}$; F. $\frac{9}{50}$, $\frac{16}{25}$, $\frac{7}{10}$, $\frac{1}{10}$

## Page 101

A. 2%, 6%, 1%, 12%; B. 37%, 69%, 40%, 21%; C. 99.9%, 49.9%, 175%, 225%; D. 0.24, 0.65, 0.88, 0.03; E. 0.17, 0.09, 0.10, 0.86; F. 0.667, 0.333, 1.45, 2.10

## Page 102

A. 0.3, 1.2, 12.8; B. 6.48, 4.8, 8.1; C. 5.44, 6.75, 38.44; D. 16, 6, 18.87; E. 2.46, 14.3, 180

## Page 103

A. $9.60, $14.40; B. $7.50, $17.50; C. $12.00, $68.00; D. $132.00, $88.00; E. $49.50, $40.50; F. $54.00, $66.00; G. $312.50, $937.50; H. $99.00, $99.00; I. $9.75, $55.25; J. $1.60, $2.40; K. $8.00, $72.00; L. $7.00, $13.00; M. $1.20, $4.80; N. $32.67, $66.33

## Page 104

A. 20, 23, 26; B. 66, 61, 56; C. 60, 52, 44; D. 50, 55, 65; E. 57, 54, 51; F. 657, 742, 827; G. 95, 131, 173; H. 172, 154, 136; I. 36, 49, 64; J. 32, 64, 128; K. 68, 74, 81; L. 70, 84, 100; M. 22, 20, 25; N. 94, 109, 124

## Page 105

A. 13, 19, 29; add 9

## Page 106

A. 16, 40, 80; multiply, four; B. 9, 11, 19, 199; 2, 1

# ANSWER KEY

## Page 107

A. 11, 14, 15; $y = x + 4$; B. 7, 8, 9; $y = x - 2$; C. 24, 28, 32; $y = 4 \cdot x$; D. 24, 30, 36; $y = 3 \cdot x$; E. 6, 7, 8; $y = x \div 2$; F. 4, 9, 20; $y = x - 1$; G. 20, 21, 22; $y = x + 15$; H. 26, 28, 30; $y = 2 \cdot x$

## Page 108

A. 8, 4; 7, 11; 6, 8; B. $y = 3$; $x = 16$; $v = 10$; $m = 6$; C. $q = 115$; $r = 56$; $w = 64$; $z = 41$; D. $a = 13$; $y = 67$; $g = 16$; $c = 107$

## Page 109

A. $t = 9$; 81, $n = 1$; 6, $y = 7$; B. $x = 4$; $v = 4$; $h = 8$; $g = 3$; C. $c = 50$; $g = 36$; $y = 1{,}875$; $s = 242$; D. $b = 4$; $f = 17$; $d = 492$; $z = 464$

## Page 110

A. $\dfrac{7}{18}$, $\dfrac{4}{9}$; B. $\dfrac{5}{6}$, $\dfrac{5}{9}$, $\dfrac{5}{9}$; C. $\dfrac{1}{6}$, $\dfrac{1}{3}$, $\dfrac{1}{2}$; D. $\dfrac{5}{6}$, $\dfrac{1}{2}$, $\dfrac{2}{3}$

## Page 111

A. mean: 36, median: 34, mode: 41, range; 10;
B. mean: 16, median: 10, mode: 10, range: 27;
C. mean: 15, median: 14, mode: 14, range: 22;
D. mean: 42, median: 41, mode: 41, range: 66

## Page 112

A. 44 green marbles; B. 540 students;
C. 160 students; D. 30 small, 90 medium, 130 large

## Page 113

A. $\dfrac{5}{7}$, $\dfrac{20}{13}$; B. $\dfrac{12}{5}$, $\dfrac{4}{9}$; C. $\dfrac{23¢}{45¢}$, $\dfrac{10}{3}$; D. $\dfrac{1}{4}$, $\dfrac{3}{25}$; E. $\dfrac{3}{3}$; F. $\dfrac{2}{3}$; G. $\dfrac{3}{3}$; H. $\dfrac{2}{8}$; I. $\dfrac{48}{54}$; J. $\dfrac{57}{104}$; K. $\dfrac{42}{104}$; L. $\dfrac{60}{44}$

## Page 114

A. $n = 54$; B. $n = 40$; C. $n = 240$, D. $n = 400$; E. $n = 12$; F. $n = 350$

## Page 115

A. $m = 4$, $a = 1$, $d = 4$, $n = 14$; B. $p = 18$, $j = 2$, $s = 20$, $y = 9$; C. $r = 1$, $k = 36$, $g = 24$, $t = 7$; D. $b = 10$, $m = 6$, $r = 12$, $n = 3$

## Page 116

A. 10,560, 15, 12; B. 5, 3, 4; C. 2, 12, 16; D. 1, 2, 11; E. 6, 48, 14,000; F. 147, 5, 1; G. <, <, >; H. <, >, <

## Page 117

A. 700, 60, 35; B. 820, 8,000, 19; C. 0.003, 450, 66; D. 4,000,000, 7.08, 35,000; E. 90, 6.8, 2,500; F. 250, 14, 520,000; G. <, >, <; H. >, >, >

## Page 118

A. 45°, acute; 130°, obtuse; 30°, acute; B. 110°, obtuse; 65°, acute; 90°, right; C. 100°, obtuse; 90°, right; 40°, acute; D. 155°, obtuse; 90°, right; 20°, acute

## Page 119

A. 40°, obtuse; 80°, acute; 90°, right; 75°, acute; B. 39°, acute; 46°, acute; 97°, obtuse; 90°, right

## Page 120

A. 54; 200; 18; B. 30; 24; 17.5; C. 40; 90; 172.2